BFI FILM CLASSICS

· ·

Rob White
SERIES EDITOR

Colin MacCabe and David Meeker
SERIES CONSULTANTS

Cinema is a fragile medium. Many of the great classic films of the past now exist, if at all, in damaged or incomplete prints. Concerned about the deterioration in the physical state of our film heritage, the National Film and Television Archive, a Division of the British Film Institute, has compiled a list of 360 key films in the history of the cinema. The long-term goal of the Archive is to build a collection of perfect showprints of these films, which will then be screened regularly at the Museum of the Moving Image in London in a year-round repertory.

BFI Film Classics is a series of books commissioned to stand alongside these titles. Authors, including film critics and scholars, film-makers, novelists, historians and those distinguished in the arts, have been invited to write on a film of their choice, drawn from the Archive's list. Each volume presents the author's own insights into the chosen film, together with a brief production history and a detailed filmography, notes and bibliography. The numerous illustrations have been specially made from the Archive's own prints.

With new titles published each year, the BFI Film Classics series will rapidly grow into an authoritative and highly readable guide to the great films of world cinema.

Could scarcely be improved upon ... informative, intelligent, jargon-free companions.
The Observer

Cannily but elegantly packaged BFI Classics will make for a neat addition to the most discerning shelves.
New Statesman & Society

BFI FILM CLASSICS

L'AVVENTURA

. . . .

Geoffrey Nowell-Smith

bfi Publishing

First published in 1997 by the
BRITISH FILM INSTITUTE
21 Stephen Street, London W1P 2LN

The British Film Institute exists
to promote appreciation, enjoyment, protection and
development of moving image culture in and throughout the
whole of the United Kingdom.
Its activities include the National Film and
Television Archive; the National Film Theatre;
the Museum of the Moving Image;
the London Film Festival; the production and
distribution of film and video; funding and support for
regional activities; Library and Information Services;
Stills, Posters and Designs; Research;
Publishing and Education; and the monthly
Sight and Sound magazine.

British Library Cataloguing-in-Publication Data
A catalogue record for this book is available from the British Library

ISBN 0–85170–534–0

Designed by
Andrew Barron & Collis Clements Associates

Typesetting by
D R Bungay Associates, Burghfield, Berks.

Printed in Great Britain by Norwich Colour Printers

CONTENTS

PREFATORY NOTE

....

Throughout this book, the titles given for films are those that are, or seem to me to be, most commonly in use in English-speaking countries. Antonioni's later films, from *The Eclipse* (*L'eclisse*, 1962) onwards, are generally referred to under their English-language titles, as are some films by other directors. Although most of Antonioni's earlier films did have translated titles assigned to them on British or American release, these titles have tended not to stick, and all of his films up to and including *La notte* (1961), and of course *L'avventura* itself, are referred to under their original titles. For further details see the filmography on p. 73.

The stills in the book are, where indicated as such, frame stills, taken from the BFI's print of the film. The remainder are production or scene stills, selected from the BFI Stills, Posters and Designs collection. The map on p. 21 is reproduced from Michele Mancini and Giuseppe Perrella, *Michelangelo Antonioni: Architetture della visione* (Rome: Coneditor, 1986).

Much of this book was written in a peaceful office put at my disposal by the European Humanities Research Centre at the University of Oxford, whom I should like to thank. The book was commissioned by Ed Buscombe, my successor at BFI Publishing. By the time it was finished, Ed had joined the exodus from the BFI,[1] and the manuscript (or computerscript) was delivered into the capable and friendly hands of Rob White. In the course of writing it I received precious help from Carlo di Carlo, and from Jack O'Connell, Sam Rohdie, Penelope Houston, Markku Salmi, and David Nowell-Smith – to all of whom thanks.

Geoffrey Nowell-Smith
London, April 1997

Noto: a small crowd of men gathers to stare at Claudia

INTRODUCTION
· ·

L'avventura is a classic. But it was not born to be a classic. In fact it was nearly not born at all, and when it was born it was nearly stifled at birth. Half-way through the filming the producers went bankrupt, leaving the director, cast and crew marooned on a barren island off the Sicilian coast. Frantic negotiations conducted on an antediluvian telephone led to the finding of a new producer, but the shooting schedule had slipped and the film was barely completed in time for its anticipated premiere at Cannes. The premiere was a disaster, with boos and catcalls erupting from parts of the auditorium. Only a concerted campaign, led by a group of mainly French critics, rescued it from the threat of instant oblivion.

Does *L'avventura* deserve classic status? Of course it does. It is a momentous film. Nearly forty years after its making it still has the power to move audiences not least with its surprising modernity. The film's reputation, and that of its director, are now secure, with a place in the history books unlikely to be much revised. Justice has been done. The dinner-jacketed loons who tried to jeer it off the screen have not had their way. But the judgment of history which protects the film from harm has a disadvantage. The film now comes gift-wrapped. It can move but it can no longer shock. But it did once shock, and it is important to know why.

I first saw *L'avventura* in Paris, in November 1960. I was a language assistant in a *lycée* in a small town in eastern France. One weekend I drove with friends to Paris – 250 kilometres in a Citroën 2 c.v., maximum speed 90 k.p.h. – intending to see Truffaut's *Shoot the Pianist*, Chabrol's *Les Bonnes femmes* and other new French films. First, however, I decided to take a look at the Italian film which had caused all that uproar at Cannes the previous spring: Michelangelo Antonioni's *L'avventura*. For two and a half hours I sat spellbound in the cinema. I was captivated by the film's lingering rhythm, its decentred images, its listless characters, and especially by Monica Vitti, the star of the film and incarnation of the director's vision. No film before or since has ever made such an impression on me as *L'avventura* did on that occasion. I saw the film again the following day, and went back to Paris three weeks later to see it again – this time with the intention of writing about it. I remember that

I also saw *Shoot the Pianist*, but I never got round to seeing *Les Bonnes femmes* and haven't to this day.

My reaction may have been extreme, but it was not – I soon discovered – untypical. I still meet people who remember it in much the same way. Audiences today are divided in their response, though few react with the mindless hostility shown by the Cannes festival audience at the premiere. Even in the disenchanted atmosphere of a university classroom, watching a scratchy 16 mm print or a flickery video, students can still be bowled over by it.

Today's audiences, however, more or less know what they are in for. They have chosen to go the local art house, to get the video on the appropriately named Connoisseur label, or – in the case of students – to sign up for the course in Italian cinema. They are seeing a classic, a film with its place in the history books, and one which might excite or might disappoint, but, cocooned as it is by the history behind it, cannot be entirely new.

Writing about *L'avventura* in a series entitled 'Film Classics' is inevitably a confirmation of its status. This in itself is no bad thing. Film history needs its triangulation points, a way of mapping the terrain from pinnacle to pinnacle. And yet I am not entirely happy with the idea of *L'avventura* as an unquestioned classic, whose status we have now got right even if it was not recognised at the time. There are some films on which the mantle of classic falls naturally and elegantly: *Ugetsu monogatari* or *Lola Montès* for example. But *L'avventura* is different. It is not a timeless masterpiece, but a masterpiece of its time, and its time was a turning point in film history. It was the beginning of an epoch, not its culmination, and it was hated as well as loved at the time it came out – as were two other equally seminal films of the period, Godard's *À bout de souffle* and Hitchcock's *Psycho*. Justifying its appeal now is only part of the story. It is also important to understand precisely what it was doing then, and what turning point it represented.

The late 1950s and early 60s were years of radical renewal in the cinema. The Hollywood studio system was in decline, and so too (for related reasons) were the traditional film-making institutions in Europe and Japan. New cinemas sprang up all over the world. In France there was the *nouvelle vague*, in Britain Free Cinema, in Germany the Young German Cinema, in Brazil Cinema Novo. The years 1959 and 1960 saw first features by François Truffaut (*Les Quatre cents coups*), Jean-Luc

Godard (*À bout de souffle*), Alain Resnais (*Hiroshima mon amour*), Karel Reisz (*Saturday Night and Sunday Morning*), John Cassavetes (*Shadows*) and Nagisa Oshima (*A Town of Love and Hope*). Within a couple of years these new directors were joined by Glauber Rocha (*Barravento*), Pier Paolo Pasolini (*Accattone*), Agnès Varda (*Cléo de 5 à 7*) and Roman Polański (*Knife in the Water*). This unparalleled explosion of new talent helped create conditions of greater freedom also for more established artists – for Ingmar Bergman in Sweden, Federico Fellini in Italy, Satyajit Ray in India, Stanley Kubrick in the United States.

Aesthetically the new cinemas were in many respects quite different, but they had in common a rebellion against the false perfection of the studio film. Their cumulative effect was to break down the traditional unspoken compact between the studio and the mass audience and replace it with a new, less stable but more explicit relationship between individual film-makers and that part of the audience that was prepared to venture with them into new and uncharted territory. The director as author acquired a new visibility. Open-ended narratives, internal quotation, autobiographical references, first-person statements, even negative devices like the absence of glitz and gloss, all drew the spectator's attention not just to the film as something that someone had made but to the someone who had made it and the proposition he or she was thereby making. Attributes which in previous decades had been distinct exceptions (in *Citizen Kane*, for example, or *Vertigo*, or *La Ronde*) now became the norm or anti-norm. For the first time since the silent period the cinema, or part of it, found itself aligned fair and square with the artistic culture of modernism.

In 1960, then, the cinema stood – or appeared to stand – on the threshold of a new world. As things turned out, the new world did not fully materialise. Old and new cinemas were forced to compromise, with the results that we see today. Of the claims staked by the new cinema many proved to be without foundation. Some films, however, more than justify the claims they made for themselves, or that were made for them, in those heady years, and *L'avventura* is one of them. It is a film whose self-presentation is quite modest. It tells a simple story, with few flourishes and a minimum of authorial intrusion. It does not seem to be setting out to *do* anything particularly original – to question conventional morality, to subvert narrative, to erode the traditional concept of character or redefine the relationship of character to landscape. And yet it is a film which promotes reflection on all these things. It is a film which makes the world look different, and after which other films look stale.

It is hard to overstate the importance of *L'avventura* when it came out in 1960. If the new cinemas in general represented a break with the academicism of the studio film comparable to that in painting begun with Courbet and consummated by the Impressionists, then Antonioni was like Cézanne, offering a vision of space, bodies and surfaces that was a revolution within a revolution, and one for which the world was not, and perhaps still is not, prepared. The feeling that *L'avventura* was a revolution in the making was widespread when it came out. Defining it was not easy. Even today it remains a hard film to write about. For the greatness of the film consists precisely in the fact that it takes the cinema's powers of expression beyond the point where language can follow it. My hope is that this book will both account for *L'avventura*, in so far as a book can do this, and will open up a path along which the film itself is the only possible guide.

1
. . . .
THE SCANDAL OF 'L'AVVENTURA'

The story of *L'avventura* is deceptively simple. A group of rich Italians is going for a cruise on a yacht off the coast of Sicily. They stop to visit a deserted volcanic island and when they re-embark on the boat they discover that one of their number, Anna (Lea Massari), is missing. Her lover Sandro (Gabriele Ferzetti) and her best friend Claudia (Monica Vitti) search for her, first on the small island, then on the mainland of Sicily. In the course of the search they fall in love themselves. This new love affair is threatened when Sandro spends a night with a society tart he had previously encountered in the search for Anna. Although distressed, Claudia seems inclined to forgive him.

A story, then, in which various things happen, but more importantly, one in which a particular thing does not happen: Anna does not reappear. Accident, kidnap, suicide, escape, whatever it was, the audience never knows. The thought that she might return casts a shadow over the relationship between Claudia and Sandro and leaves the audience in suspense. This is not positive suspense *à la* Hitchcock, which mounts to a climax and is then resolved. It is a negative, nagging suspense, an absence in the plot which is never filled.

Not only does the audience never find out what happened to Anna. In all probability the director didn't know either, or, more to the point, didn't care. That is to say, we are not dealing with a piece of information which is artfully withheld, but with one which simply does not exist. There is no resolution to the story of Anna's disappearance; not in the film, nor in any statement made by Antonioni before or after the film was made. The question of what happens to Anna not only is not answered but, more radically, cannot be answered, since there is nowhere to turn for an answer. This is disconcerting, all the more so because this is a fiction, and in fiction one expects answers. In real life, if someone disappeared, then one could say that something had happened to her, even if one didn't know what. But a fictional character who goes missing in this way disappears absolutely, because she has no existence outside the story. The first challenge posed by *L'avventura* is how to cope with the radical nature of this absence.

The audience which booed *L'avventura* at Cannes was not merely bored. It was angry. It was angry because the plot did not do what a plot is supposed to do and answer what it appeared to have set up as its principal question. It was doubly angry because the character who disappeared was played by Lea Massari, a fairly well known and popular actress who most people would have expected to be the star. As the film proceeds centre stage is instead taken by the slightly horse-faced woman who shares the billing on the credits, the unknown Monica Vitti. Deprived of its heroine, the audience (or sections of it) became increasingly restive. The catcalls reached a crescendo at the end when the film reached the nearest thing that it comes to certainty – that the hero would be reconciled to the wrong woman. That was, and is, the public face of the 'scandal' of *L'avventura*.

Did Antonioni know that this would be the public's first reaction to his film? At one level, he must have done. He knew he was taking a risk. The original producers of the film, who in this respect at least knew their business as purveyors of what the public would expect, wanted the story to end with a resolution. Reluctantly, Antonioni was prepared to offer one: Claudia would learn, near the end of the film, that Anna was dead. This would provide an ending, albeit an unhappy one. It would solve the intellectual expectations of this (or any other) plot, if not the emotional demands of that particular audience. But he had no wish to deliver on his offer and when the film went into production he was planning two versions of the end, one to appease the producers and one to satisfy himself. When the first producers went bankrupt he got agreement from the new producer, Cino Del Duca, that the end should be as he wanted it. The crisis that overcame the film in mid-production was a blessing in disguise. If the film had been finished and shown as the original producers hoped, it would have avoided a scandal, but it would have been a lesser film. In the event, the film was awarded a special prize by the critics at Cannes – 'for its search for a new cinematic language and for the beauty of its images' – and this endorsement was confirmed when it went on to run in Paris for three solid months. Fortified by this endorsement, Antonioni was able, two years later, to push back the boundaries of acceptable film narration even further and to deceive even more boldly the expectations of the audience with the ending of *The Eclipse*, where only the camera turns up to keep the appointment the characters have made.

The steps that Antonioni would take in the future, or those that other film-makers would take following in his footsteps, could not however have been foreseen in the Palais des Festivaux at Cannes, on the evening of 15 May 1960, when Antonioni fled in tears from the onslaught of the philistines.

2

. . . .

THE DIRECTOR

At the time of the fateful showing of *L'avventura* in Cannes Antonioni was forty-six years old. He was born in Ferrara, in the Po Valley, on 29 September 1913. He had a conventional education suited to his bourgeois background, graduating from the University of Bologna in Economics and Commerce in 1935. Over the next four years he wrote regular film criticism for the local Ferrara newspaper, the *Corriere Padano*. In 1940 he moved to Rome, enrolling at the recently founded state film school, the Centro Nazionale di Cinematografia. There he came into contact with the young dissidents around the magazine *Cinema*, to which he became a contributor. He wrote or collaborated on a couple of screenplays, including Rossellini's *Un pilota ritorna* of 1942. In the same year he paid a visit to Nice on behalf of the Italian company Scalera and acted as an assistant on Marcel Carné's *Les Visiteurs du soir*. Back in Italy, he returned (as he would often do throughout his life) to his home territory near Ferrara with plans to shoot a documentary about the people of the Po Valley. The success of the Allied invasion of Italy in the summer of 1943 meant that shooting had to be interrupted. When he reclaimed his footage after the war, he found that much of it had perished, but he finished the film none the less, under the title *Gente del Po*, in 1947. It is a remarkable film, in many ways prefiguring his later work.[2] He then made a number of other short documentaries, all interesting, but none perhaps quite as striking as his first effort, while awaiting the chance to shoot a feature.

This chance came to him in 1950. The Italian cinema was beginning to recover from the body-blows dealt to it, first by the war and then, even more seriously, by the deluge of American films that flooded the market after the war was over. The gap between the collapse of the Fascist film industry and the gradual resurgence of a post-war commercial industry had been filled by neo-realism, a politico-aesthetic movement which stressed working-class subject matter, shooting in real locations, simplicity of means, and narrative which eschewed the foregone conclusions of melodrama.[3] By 1950 the neo-realist movement was on the wane. Antonioni had always stood aloof from neo-realism and even when he agreed with its methods or objectives (the preference for location shooting, for example) he did so for different reasons. Even allowing for this separateness, Antonioni's first feature, *Cronaca di un amore* ('Story of a love affair'), first shown in October 1950, came as a shock.

Cronaca di un amore is a tale about two former lovers who are brought together again when the woman's millionaire husband hires a private detective to investigate her past. With its film noir plot and its wealthy bourgeois setting, all furs and fast cars, and with its elaborate and self-conscious camera movements, *Cronaca di un amore* could hardly be further, in style or content, from the world of neo-realism as represented by such films as Visconti's *La terra trema* or De Sica and Zavattini's *Bicycle Thieves*.

Nor, however, did *Cronaca* (or any of Antonioni's subsequent features) fit comfortably into the world of the resurgent commercial industry or the popular marketplace where Italian and American genre films jostled for public attention. The film is neither thrilling nor

Massimo Girotti and Lucia Bosè as the guilty lovers in Antonioni's first feature, *Cronaca di un amore* (1950)

Lucia Bosè in *La signora senza camelie* (1953)

Valentina Cortese and Madeleine Fisher in *Le amiche* (1955)

Steve Cochran and Alida Valli in *Il grido* (1957)

melodramatic. The plot lacks a climax. The noir atmosphere peters out into vague shades of grey. The lovers' crisis is expressed more as an ill-defined malaise than as cathartic suffering. In short, it lacked any of the qualities that would make it fit with either critical or audience expectations. It was a film literally *sui generis* – in a genre of its own – and as such little appreciated on first release.[4]

After *Cronaca*, Antonioni was commissioned in 1952 by a producer to direct a film about the 'problem' of juvenile delinquency. The result, *I vinti* ('The vanquished', also known as *These Our Children*) was competent, but did little for the director's reputation. Far more important were his next two films, *La signora senza camelie* ('The lady without camellias', 1953), and *Le amiche* ('The girl-friends', 1955).

In *La signora senza camelie*, Lucia Bosè (the lead actress from *Cronaca*) plays the role of a shop-girl, Clara, precipitated into stardom by a film industry eager for profits and prestige and unceremoniously dumped when she proves not to be up to what is required. Truly the stuff of melodrama – but equally a possible subject for social realism. Antonioni offers neither. Clara's background is not explored in depth, nor are the commercial mechanisms of the industry which uses and abuses her. Clara is not really defined as a character, at least not in the sense of fitting into a repertory of character types. Instead Antonioni creates a set of arabesques around the extraordinarily beautiful figure of Bosè which gradually accumulate until at the end Clara's tragedy is both moving and credible – more so than, for example, that of the Lana Turner character in Minnelli's *The Bad and the Beautiful*, released the previous year.

The social rise of a working girl is again the theme (or one of the themes) of *Le amiche*, and again it is not exploited. *Le amiche* is an adaptation (by Antonioni and two women writers, Suso Cecchi D'Amico and Alba De Cespedes) of Cesare Pavese's novel *Tra donne sole*. Clelia (played in the film by Eleonora Rossi Drago), who has risen to become the manager of a leading fashion house in Rome, returns to her home city of Turin to open a branch of the company there. She falls in with a group of artists and socialites, but never feels part of them. Instead she is attracted to Carlo, the foreman overseeing construction of the new atelier and showroom, who represents the world of her origins. After the eruption of various personal crises in the world around her, things turn out badly for Clelia, and she goes back to Rome to resume her career, leaving Carlo behind.

A number of features of *Le amiche* prefigure *L'avventura*. Like Claudia in the later film, Clelia is an observer of a world to which she does not fully belong. Lorenzo, the character played by Gabriele Ferzetti, exemplifies traits of an apparently self-confident masculinity masking an insecure core which the same actor brings to the portrayal of Sandro in *L'avventura*. And an extraordinary sequence in which the characters take a trip to the seaside and wander around a beach while the camera follows their interaction clearly anticipates the island sequences in the later film.

With *Le amiche* Antonioni definitively established himself as a director of international renown. The film won a Silver Lion at Venice and performed more than respectably at the box office. It was released in Paris in 1957 and championed by *Positif*. By this time Antonioni was on to his next and perhaps least appreciated film, *Il grido* ('The cry'). For the first time since his early documentaries, Antonioni opted to abandon the world of the bourgeoisie and set the film in a working-class environment. Aldo (played by Steve Cochran, an odd but inspired choice) is a worker in a sugar refinery, whose life is thrown into crisis when he discovers that the woman he lives with no longer loves him. The film consists of Aldo's wanderings, from place to place and from woman to woman, until a final, disastrous accident leads to his death.

The critics were puzzled by *Il grido*. To some it seemed like a throw-back to neo-realism, to others more like a caricature. In fact it was neither, though this fact was slow to permeate. A Critics' Prize at Locarno and a handful of sympathetic reviews were not enough to enable the film to make an impact. But critical opinion had gradually shifted Antonioni's way. The reviews he was getting were more respectful, if not enthusiastic. The cultural climate was changing, not only in Italy but also in France, where the *nouvelle vague* was about to burst from its cocoon. Whatever film Antonioni made after *Il grido* could well be a turning point. But first he had to make it.

3

....

THE ADVENTURE OF 'L'AVVENTURA'

As often with Antonioni's films, the idea for *L'avventura* took off from a chance event. As he himself describes it:

I remember very well how the idea for *L'avventura* came to me. I was on a yacht with some friends, and I used to wake up first and sit on the front deck and let my thoughts roam. One morning I found myself thinking about a girl who had disappeared some years back and who had not been heard of since. We had looked for her everywhere for days and days, to no avail. The yacht was sailing towards Ponza [an island off the west coast of Italy, between Rome and Naples], which we were just approaching. And I thought: suppose she's there? That was it.

However fascinating I find an idea, though, I can't accept it immediately. I leave it there, don't think about it, just wait. Months, even years, go by. It has to keep floating in the sea of things that pile up in the course of life; if it does, it's a good idea.[5]

Not only does the idea have to prove itself as an idea, it also has to become first a script and then a film. This process can be laborious. Antonioni started preparatory work on *L'avventura* shortly after finishing *Il grido* in 1957. For script collaborators he chose Elio Bartolini, who had worked with him on *Il grido* and was also a novelist, and Tonino Guerra, who was to work with him on many subsequent films up to *Beyond the Clouds* but who was better known at the time as a poet and novelist than for his work as a scriptwriter. As producers of the film, Antonioni found a company called Imeria, which was eager to invest money in film production. As things turned out, this was an unwise choice.

Antonioni wanted (as was his usual custom) to shoot the entire film on location. There therefore had to be a lot of toing and froing while locations were found for scenes to be shot in and scenes were adjusted to suit the location. Eventually the makings of a shooting script emerged. It involved an opening sequence in Rome, in which the main characters were introduced. The rest of the film was to be shot in Sicily and in or around the Aeolian Islands off the north coast. The cruise party lands on one of the smallest of these islands, called Lisca Bianca, where Anna disappears. Having searched ineffectually for Anna on Lisca Bianca, the party repairs to the mainland. Here various locations were envisaged. A scene where Anna's disappearance was reported to the police, set in the port of Milazzo, the nearest mainland town to the Aeolian islands, was to be shot in an eighteenth-century villa converted to offices in a place called Bagheria further to the west. Another villa near Palermo, home of a branch of the Lampedusa family, was needed for a scene in which Claudia, waiting for news from Sandro, witnesses the willing seduction of one of the cruise party by a young painter.

Claudia and Sandro then embark on the second phase of the search, following up a lead provided by a local journalist. They set out into the interior, to a village called Troina, where they are directed to Noto, a baroque town on the east coast. En route they come to a deserted village called Santa Panagia, near the coast, which is where they fall in love. After spending the night in Noto, where a number of locations were called for, Sandro and Claudia head north again. In an early version of the script Sandro's betrayal of Claudia was planned to be set in a small hotel near the resort town of Taormina, but in the final version it takes

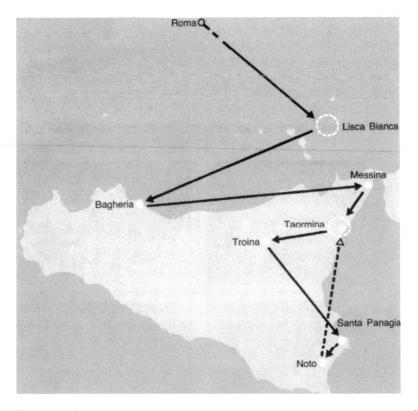

place in the luxurious San Domenico Palace in Taormina itself, and the other woman is not just a local prostitute but an American woman, a self-styled writer, whom Sandro has previously caught sight of when questioning the journalist. Deciding on this second ending meant that a further scene had to be added, in the provincial capital of Messina, where Gloria, as the woman calls herself, is mobbed by a crowd of men. With the itinerary mapped out and its budgetary implications analysed, it was time to engage cast and crew. For director of photography the natural choice would have been Gianni Di Venanzo, the great black-and-white cinematographer who had shot *Le amiche* and *Il grido* and would go on to shoot *La notte* and *The Eclipse*. Since he was not available, Antonioni opted for Aldo Scavarda, who had been the camera operator and assistant to Enzo Serafin on *Cronaca di un amore*, *I vinti* and *La signora senza camelie* and with Serafin had pioneered the use of diffused lighting effects that Antonioni preferred. For the art direction Antonioni chose Piero Poletto, a relative newcomer, who was later to perform the same role on *The Eclipse*, *Red Desert* and *The Passenger*. The job of art director was to prove particularly taxing in the improvised and often bizarre conditions which were to prevail during the shooting.

For the cast Antonioni engaged the distinguished theatre actor Renzo Ricci in the relatively minor role of Anna's father. Lea Massari as Anna and Gabriele Ferzetti as Sandro were also fairly well known, and Ferzetti had worked with Antonioni before on *Le amiche*. The remaining roles were filled unsystematically. Dominique Blanchar, daughter of the great Pierre Blanchar and no mean actress in her own right, plays Giulia, the woman who is seduced by the young painter. Conversely, Giulia's long-standing partner Corrado is played by James Addams, a retired US colonel and father of the film star Dawn Addams. (The fact that Colonel Addams was neither an actor nor an Italian speaker was not an obstacle, since his voice would be dubbed in the studio.) Other roles were filled with a selection of professionals and non-professionals. The major surprise in the casting was Antonioni's choice for the role of Claudia. Monica Vitti was a versatile theatre actress, but unknown in the cinema. Antonioni had seen her perform and had been captivated both by her acting and by her personality. As he came to know her, he came more and more to construct the part around her. It is hard now to imagine the role performed by anyone else. But there is no doubt that at the time

Antonioni was taking a great risk in employing this untried and unknown young woman in the role.

The plan was to shoot the entire film, not only on location, but as far as possible in continuity. Shooting began in August 1959, in Rome. A schedule was mapped out which envisaged completing the island sequences in September and then proceeding to mainland Sicily in early autumn. All being well, the whole film could be in the can around Christmas.

All was not well. Things began to go wrong in Rome. Only two sequences were needed: one, very brief, in which Anna says goodbye to her father before setting out on the cruise and in which Claudia also appears; and one, more elaborate, in which Claudia is kept waiting outside while Anna goes up to Sandro's flat to collect him, and the couple stop to make love.

At the time the shooting script was finished, no location had been decided on for this second sequence. But an opportunity arose to borrow an apartment on the Isola Tiberina in the old centre of Rome, belonging to a certain Lady Montague, who had been the confidante of Princess Margaret and Group Captain Peter Townsend at the time of their liaison five years earlier. In her ladyship's absence, the production crew turned the apartment upside down, clamping lights and reflectors into the walls and leaving the place, in a crew member's words, 'like a battlefield'.[6] Another scene was also improvised, in which Claudia, waiting for Anna and Sandro, wanders into an art gallery and listens to a pretentious American praising some paintings and a down-to-earth Roman dismissing them. All this took far longer to shoot than had been anticipated, though the main sufferer was Lady Montague and the house guest she was about to entertain, Lady Diana Cooper.

It was not until the end of August, already somewhat delayed, that Poletto and his team arrived on Lisca Bianca, to supervise the arrival of the equipment and the construction of the shepherd's hut in which Claudia, Sandro and Corrado take shelter during the search for Anna. Antonioni, the rest of the crew, and the cast, arrived on 14 September to find the hut not yet built, the wrong weather, and no yacht for the cruise party to disport themselves on – or to transport them to and from the larger island, Panarea, on which they would be staying.

In the absence of a yacht, the swimming sequences – for which the weather would have been perfect – had to be delayed. In the event they

24   Michelangelo Antonioni with Monica Vitti during the shooting of *L'avventura*

were not shot until November, by which time the water had got cold and the light had become autumnal. (This had a compensation, in that the autumn light gives an eerie quality to the swimming sequences which would not have been achieved in September.) Meanwhile the still water and cloudless September skies meant that the scenes surrounding Anna's disappearance, which required menacing weather, could not be shot either. Nor could the scene in the hut.

Abandoning hope of shooting in continuity, Antonioni started with the now famous scenes of the cruise party wandering incongruously around the island, looking for Anna. Other scenes were shot as and when circumstances permitted. Cast and crew were lodged on Panarea, in bug-ridden accommodation, and ferried to and from Lisca Bianca on a fishing boat.

The bad weather came eventually, with a vengeance. A sudden storm left cast and crew marooned overnight on Lisca Bianca and broke the improvised pontoons on which the lights, generators, and camera-tracks were stored, throwing vital equipment into the sea, from which it had to be rescued by divers. When the yacht arrived, it turned out to be a 40-footer, and far too small either as a transport or as a location for the scenes to be shot on it, some of which had to be deferred.

As Antonioni struggled to get as many scenes safely in the can as he possibly could, a fresh disaster struck. The money from the producers, needed to pay the lodging-house keepers, failed to turn up. News followed that the production house, Imeria, had gone bankrupt. Antonioni called a meeting of the entire company and begged for support. The local big-shot, and owner of Panarea's only restaurant, agreed to accept credit, provided nobody left the island until he was paid back. The crew went on strike. Members of the cast threw tantrums, and only Monica Vitti preserved her calm and good humour. Frantic appeals to Rome were issued, using the only available means of communication, an antique two-way radio. Then a message came through that a reputable producer, Cino Del Duca, was prepared in principle to take over the production. The message was followed by an emissary of the company, who disembarked on the island, spent three days negotiating with Antonioni, and departed with a promise. Two weeks later he returned with a leather briefcase bulging with cash and cheques. The production was saved. Lea Massari meanwhile had suffered a heart attack and kidney failure and had to be helicoptered back to Rome. The rest of the company prepared to move to the Sicilian mainland to shoot the rest of the film.

Although the production was saved, it was running desperately behind schedule. Renzo Ricci's contract had expired and he was not available for the scene in the police station where Anna's disappearance was reported. A couple of lines of new dialogue were concocted (though never actually used) to cover his absence: 'Where is His Excellency?', 'In the next room, making a phone call.' The weather was a further problem. It was not until after Christmas that Antonioni got round to shooting the scene where Gloria is mobbed by a crowd of randy Sicilian men, and a couple of hundred extras had to be persuaded to run around in shirtsleeves pretending it was summer, though the temperature was barely above freezing. The oranges had ripened on the trees, and Antonioni took it into his head to add a scene in which Claudia asked Sandro to pick her an orange. Preparations were made to shoot it, but overnight the farmer came and harvested the crop, so oranges had to be hung on the tree with bits of wire. The scene was never used, which is probably just as well, since the pretence was maintained that action takes place in late summer, when the oranges are not ripe.

In spite of everything, Antonioni remained not only optimistic but obstinate. The love scene outside the village of Santa Panagia takes place by a railway line. Ten days were needed to shoot the scene, because the express train which disturbs the lovers comes only once a day and retakes had to be timed for its passing. The decision to shoot the finale in the San Domenico Palace, rather than in a smaller place nearby, also created complications. The scenes in the hotel needed a large cast and elaborate orchestration. But the hotel was doing normal business, and the public rooms were only available in the small hours, when the regular guests had gone to bed. There were also missing bits to fill in. Besides the scene on the yacht, where Sandro makes a first attempt to kiss Claudia and which was finally shot on an ex-Royal Navy torpedo boat in Palermo harbour, there were some scenes on Lisca Bianca to be completed. Again this had to be done in the dead of winter.

Apart from the harassed production team, the person whose job was made particularly difficult by conditions was the script supervisor, Elvira D'Amico. She had to keep a log of all the scenes that were not shot at the right time and all the matches that had to be made between shots – many of these shots having been improvised and not foreseen in any continuity script. Moreover, throughout the shooting, and especially for the island sequences, there was no system for viewing daily rushes. Under the circumstances it was a near miracle that, when Antonioni got back to Rome, he found enough material to enable him and his editor Eraldo Da Roma to edit the film into shape. According to Jack O'Connell, Antonioni's assistant on the production, only one shot needed to be retaken in the studio, a tiny cutaway.[7]

Back in Rome, Da Roma and Antonioni worked on giving the film not only shape but rhythm. A certain amount of material was discarded because it was superfluous to the narrative and the film was already very long. But a number of scenes were allowed to develop at their own pace, unrestricted by the pressure of narrative. This is most apparent in the island sequences, surrounding the disappearance of Anna. As if to emphasise the fact that the disappearance was not so much an event as a non-event (Anna has not done anything, she is just not there), it is accompanied by scenes in which the characters walk around, exchange commonplaces, and generally do nothing much. It is only when a storm gets up, and the thought impinges that she might have drowned, that the film recovers narrative force. Here Antonioni and Da Roma stretch out the sequences, giving a sense of indefinite time, rather than time defined by action. Match cuts are in any case rare in Antonioni films and footage of each take extends at each end beyond what is strictly necessary for the action. Shots were also used with no human action at all, just empty landscape in which nature alone is the protagonist.

Once a rough cut was put together, the sound track had to be made. This involved recalling some of the actors and bringing in specialist dubbers for those whose voices were not needed. An effects track also had to be generated, mostly of sound created in the studio.

For the music, finally, Antonioni turned, as he had done for almost all his previous films, to Giovanni Fusco. Fusco's scores for Antonioni are generally sparse, almost minimalist, with simple motifs and little orchestration. For *L'avventura*, Antonioni told Fusco, 'I should like a tiny orchestra: a clarinet, a saxophone, and something sounding like a drum-kit. The style should be jazz, but not exactly jazz. Imagine how the classical Greeks might have written a jazz score, if jazz had existed in those days.'[8]

Fusco obliged with a suite of short pieces, scored mainly for woodwind, and sufficient to occupy forty minutes of screen time. This was more than Antonioni wanted, and most of it was discarded, including the only jazzy piece. Except for a bolero used when Claudia is at the villa near Palermo, a pop song listened to by Claudia in Noto, and a piece played on-screen by a small orchestra at the San Domenico Palace near the end, most of the music finally used in the film is austere, with jagged rhythms and strange dissonances.

By April 1960 the film was ready to be shown, in time, but only just, for its scheduled encounter with press and public on 15 May.

4
. . . .

A VIEWING

In its finished form, *L'avventura* runs for 145 minutes. It is in black and white and in a non-anamorphic widescreen format with an aspect ratio of 1.85:1.[9] The film opens with the credits, bold white on black. Over the credits runs some insistent music, scored for plucked instruments – guitars or, more probably, mandolins amplified to produce a guitar-like sound. The music fades away on the last credit and the action begins. Anna appears, coming out of a courtyard. A man's voice is heard, that of Anna's father talking to a workman. The setting is in the outskirts of Rome, in an area steadily being eaten up by new housing. A slightly tense conversation ensues between father and daughter, interrupted by the arrival of Claudia. The two women and a chauffeur get into a car. There is a dissolve and the car is seen driving down the via Giulia in the old centre of Rome, then a cut to a small square. The car enters, the women get out and Anna dismisses the chauffeur. Impulsively, Anna tells Claudia that maybe she won't go on the projected cruise after all, but it is too late: Sandro has seen her from the window of his apartment overlooking the square. Anna goes upstairs to collect him. It emerges that the couple have been apart, at her insistence, for a while and that she is apprehensive about renewing the relationship. The couple make love while Claudia walks up and down outside, visits an art gallery, stands in the doorway below the apartment. Another dissolve and the characters are in a car, being driven by Sandro at breakneck speed. There is a fade to black and when the picture returns, it is of a calm sea with a conical island rising up in the left background.

The scenes in Rome have taken just over eight minutes. They have established the characters of Anna and Sandro and assigned a role, though not yet a character, to Claudia. Claudia's personality will be thrown into sharper relief in the scenes that follow. These opening scenes have also established a style. There has been no accompanying music, and there won't be any for another twenty minutes. The soundtrack is generally subdued, foregrounding only a handful of background noises and with the dialogue pitched at conversational level. Though there is some cross-cutting, there are also a number of long takes with elaborate reframings to encompass the movement of the action. This style will be maintained throughout the film.

The next sequence takes place on a yacht. Some more characters are introduced. There is the indolent Patrizia; Raimondo, her admirer; and an incongruous couple formed by the cynical Corrado and the rather silly Giulia. Some of the company decide to go swimming from the yacht. Anna creates a panic by claiming to have seen a shark. The party disembarks on the island of Lisca Bianca, where Anna and Sandro have a row. A storm is brewing, sea-swell is visible and the sound of the waves is brought into relief. When the party is about to re-embark Anna is found to be missing. The characters wander around the island calling out ineffectually. For the first time since the credits a little background music, scored for a small wind ensemble, infiltrates the soundtrack. The weather is now very menacing. Sandro, Corrado and Claudia decide to remain overnight on the island. They take shelter in a hut and are disturbed before dawn by the arrival of its owner, a shepherd, who entertains them with talk (in English) about his family in Australia but who has no useful information.[10]

The search sequence is one of the most memorable in the film and generates a distinct sense of unease in admirers and detractors alike. The characters criss-cross the screen, often being shown moving or looking away from the camera. Looks do not engage, conversations are disjointed. The landscape is a constant presence, its changing moods subtly foregrounded by the soundtrack and *mise-en-scène*.

The following morning the search is resumed. A police rescue team arrives, followed by Anna's father in a hydrofoil, followed by a helicopter. Still nothing. The action shifts to the town of Milazzo, on the Sicilian mainland, where the police interrogate some petty smugglers. We are now approximately an hour into the film. Just before leaving the

Anna (Lea Massari) with her father (Renzo Ricci) in the opening scene of the film

Rome sequence: Anna with Claudia (Monica Vitti)

... and with Sandro (Gabriele Ferzetti)

On the yacht: the indolent Patrizia (Esmeralda Ruspoli) undergoes the attentions of
her admirer Raimondo (Lelio Luttazzi)

island Sandro attempts to kiss Claudia, and he tries again to attach himself to her in Milazzo. He boards the train taking her to the villa of their friends the Montaldos, but she makes him get off. Sandro goes to Messina to meet Zuria, a local journalist, and witnesses the mobbing of Gloria who has taken refuge in a shop to buy some thread to stitch up her dress which has mysteriously come apart. Claudia meanwhile is at the villa, where she witnesses the love scene between Giulia and the young painter, set in his studio full of ugly nudes. Claudia then sets out to join Sandro, whose enquiries have led him to Troina whence a squabbling couple composed of the village pharmacist and his wife redirect him and Claudia to Noto.

On the way to Noto, Sandro and Claudia turn up in a village which proves to be quite deserted. They walk around, call out, but hear nothing but the echo of their own voices. They make their way back towards the car, and there is then a cut to the couple making love in a field, with a railway line nearby and beyond the railway a glimpse of the sea. They drive on to Noto, where Claudia is eyed up and down by a group of silent men while Sandro checks out a hotel which Anna might be staying in. Claudia and Sandro climb up a church tower where they accidentally set the bells ringing. They retire to the hotel and Claudia dances ecstatically to a pop song coming from an unseen radio. She tries to get Sandro to say he loves her, which he cannot quite bring himself to do. Sandro goes out for a further look at the baroque wonders of the town. A young student has been making a careful pen-and-ink sketch of an architectural detail. While the boy's back is turned, Sandro accidentally-on-purpose knocks over the ink bottle, and a fight threatens to break out. Back in the hotel, Claudia reveals her continuing anxiety about Anna. Sandro is less concerned, but he has a business meeting to attend with Patrizia's husband Ettore for whom he works as an estimator, so the couple agree to pack up and leave.

The couple arrive at the San Domenico Palace. Patrizia and Ettore are there. Claudia decides to retire to bed early. As Sandro says goodnight to her the music from the opening credits returns, but slower and softer and with a distinct mandolin timbre. Sandro sees Ettore, exchanges glances with Gloria, then with a girl who is standing in front of an allegorical painting, and then with Gloria again. He sits for a while watching the television. Claudia cannot sleep. She goes to see Patrizia, to discover if Sandro is with Ettore. She expresses to Patrizia her anxiety

Island sequence: left to right, Giulia (Dominique Blanchar), Corrado (James Addams), Sandro (Gabriele Ferzetti), and Patrizia (Esmeralda Ruspoli)

Sandro and Claudia in the train

3 4   Taormina dawn: Claudia waiting for Sandro ... and going in search of him (frame stills)

that Sandro might be with Anna and her sense of guilt that she no longer wants Anna to come back. She then sets out to look for Sandro and finds him on a sofa in one of the deserted lounges. He is with Gloria. Claudia runs out and a dishevelled Sandro disengages himself from Gloria who asks him for a memento of their night together. This is the last line spoken in the film. Sandro lets a couple of large banknotes flutter down on to the sofa, where Gloria collects them with her feet.

Claudia runs through the hotel gate and out into an empty car park overlooking the sea. From this point on, the film lasts just over four minutes. There are seventeen shots, all fixed-angle (except for a couple of small tilt movements). Claudia stands for a while sobbing in the car park. Sandro comes out looking for her, and sits down on a bench crying. Claudia approaches him from behind and in a final alternation of shots her hand can be seen slowly coming up to caress his shoulder and then his hair. The last shot shows her standing over him, with Mount Etna in the background. Half way through the sequence the on-screen sound has been replaced by music – a flute, a clarinet and a cor anglais or bassoon, accompanied by a kettle drum. The music continues for a few seconds over the end title, with a long drawn-out dissonant chord.

5

....

THE WORLD OF 'L'AVVENTURA'

The dissonant chord which concludes *L'avventura* says it all, or nearly all. The film is a love story. But it is one which ends with the lovers not marching into the sunset but facing an uncertain dawn. Just as the final chord – a major seventh – does not resolve but remains agonisingly poised, so Claudia's and Sandro's relationship is also on a knife-edge. To the uncertainty of what has happened to Anna is added the uncertainty of whether Claudia's and Sandro's affair has any future. It is not a happy end, but not a tragic one either. The flux of life has been halted at a particular moment, in what James Joyce called an epiphany. Life will resume its flux; it is just the story which has ended at this moment.

Stories are not everything, and *L'avventura*, like most films of substance, is not just a story. The universe it creates has a consistency which is only partly dependent on the events that form its plot and, as it happens, terminate at a particular point. Of course the characters' destiny, as revealed (to the extent that it *is* revealed) at the end of the film, is important, but no films – even Hitchcock films – exist solely to be concluded.

As well as a love story, *L'avventura* is a film about consciousness and its objects, the consciousness that people have of other people and of the environment that surrounds them. At the centre is Claudia, and radiating out from her are her immediate circle, wider society, the built environment, and on the outside, nature. The natural environment is indifferent, sometimes seen as benign, but more often as hostile. The hostile aspect is most apparent in the island sequences. The sun beats down on a barren soil, waves crash against rocks, wind whips up a waterspout. The island is uninhabited, except by a solitary shepherd (we never see his sheep). Even on the mainland there are no cultivated fields, and gardens exist only in the immediate vicinity of houses. Landscape is pure, distant, objectified. Human activity is reflected in a built environment, separated from nature, but itself objectified. The first scene of the film shows suburban sprawl engulfing the outskirts of Rome. Later, the deserted village imposes an alien rectangular geometry on the hill side on which it is incongruously situated. No grass grows in

Goffredo ('no landscape is as beautiful as a woman') in his studio with Giulia (Dominique Blanchar)

its empty streets. The baroque façades of Noto are a decaying monument. Perceived by Sandro as an emblem of a civilisation at ease with itself, they also represent a past which, like that of the deserted village, has been relegated to a liminal status, between the natural and the human.

Human society – at least as encountered by Claudia and the group – is fragmented and discontinuous. The old man on the island shows pictures of his family in Australia. A police diver talks about the history of Roman settlement in the area. A crowd of men emerges from nowhere to mob Gloria and a similar, but smaller, crowd gathers to stare at Claudia. A travelling salesman chats up a girl on a train. The couple in the village pharmacy squabble pathetically. A nun lets Sandro and Claudia play with the bell ropes in Noto. In the hotel at Taormina the girl standing in front of the picture looks come-hitherishly at Sandro, but it's not her day and she gets no response. The central characters see the social world around them, but it is a fragmentary world, observed by the director on their behalf, and impinges on them very little.

As for the characters in the central group, they too are observed, but not explained. Who are they? On the cruise there are seven of them. There is Claudia, very much outside the rest of the group. There is Anna, the diplomat's daughter; and there is Sandro, her lover, who, it appears (we only learn this later), trained as an architect and works as an estimator or quantity surveyor. Then there are the minor ones: Patrizia, rich, indolent, and married to the property developer for whom Sandro does calculations; Raimondo, the ageing toy-boy paying unsuccessful court to Patrizia and even more indolent than she is. And there is the not-actually-married couple formed by the sour but witty Corrado and the ineffably silly Giulia who eventually enjoys her revenge on him by getting off with the young painter Goffredo. Delicate portraits are drawn of each of the minor characters in the group. But they are floaters, coming from nowhere in particular and going nowhere. If they have a destiny, the film is not interested in it. The last we see of Raimondo is when he distractedly drops an antique vase found on the island. The last we see of Corrado and Giulia is when they drift off, with Goffredo, to dinner somewhere, and Corrado closes the incident with a cryptic reference to Oscar Wilde.[11] Only Patrizia reappears at the end, in Taormina, when she shows herself to be a person (as, indeed, Corrado also is) of insight and compassion.

The interiority of the minor characters is not explored. For the purposes of the film they are what Claudia and the audience see them to be. Anna and Sandro are constructed in more depth. Anna is restless and inarticulate. Her feelings are opaque. When her father turns up on the island after her disappearance, Claudia hands him two books found in her belongings: a Bible and Scott Fitzgerald's *Tender Is the Night*. The father opts for the former, concluding piously that it proves she would not have committed suicide. The film, however, suggests that the novel is a better guide, that she is like a character in *Tender Is the Night* or *The Last Tycoon*, struggling to find herself. (And, like Fitzgerald, Antonioni withholds from the audience any judgment as to what might be there to be found.) Whatever is tormenting Anna, she is unable to explain it, least of all to Sandro whose capacity for emotional understanding is strictly limited. When she disappears it is as if the group had been relieved of a burden. She had radiated an unhappiness which nobody could relate to, and she disappears from the scene almost as it she had never been there. At the end of *The Passenger*, when David Locke's wife is asked to identify his corpse, she pronounces the words, 'I never knew him.' The same could be said of Anna: nobody knew her, and only Claudia remains troubled by her loss.

Sandro is a more transparent character. He too is restless, but he is more articulate than Anna and is allowed space to explain himself. We learn that he had been ambitious but lazy and abandoned architecture when he discovered he could earn more money more easily doing sums for Ettore. His frustration with himself bursts out when he sees the student making his careful pen-and-ink drawing of the church in Noto. Having knocked over the young man's ink bottle he seems quite prepared to let the matter be resolved by a fist fight, and equally prepared to let matters rest. Sporadic acts of violence aside, however, his main way of relating to the world is through women. He resents Anna's wish for a respite from their relationship and her reluctance to resume it. His immediate response to her disappearance is to turn his attentions to Claudia – though it is not clear whether he is in a sense reclaiming Anna's shadow (when he first kisses Claudia she has been wearing a shirt given to her by Anna) or is just moving on to a new object. But move on he does, first to Claudia and then, by way of distraction, to his one-night-stand with Gloria. Like Anna, Sandro cannot account for his motives. But unlike her,

Framed in the landscape: Claudia in Goffredo's studio (frame still)

Claudia (frame still)

he has rationalisations at the ready, to satisfy other people, if not himself.

The centre of all these circles – nature, built environment, social world, group, protagonists – is Claudia. That she is going to be the centre of the film is not immediately obvious. At first sight the heroine would appear to be Anna, played by the relatively well known Lea Massari, rather than Claudia, in the person of the unknown Monica Vitti. It is Anna whose character is established first, in conversation with her father. The figure of Claudia then appears, crossing the screen from right to left behind Anna and her father. The camera reframes to bring her back into shot, but she is clearly set up as a bystander. And she remains an observer and a bystander when she is left waiting outside in the square while Anna and Sandro make love in his apartment. On the cruise and on the island when Anna disappears she is still an observer, even as she comes to assume a more dynamic role in the plot. She watches – at first amused and then horrified – as Giulia and Goffredo's flirtation turns into passionate grappling and groping. Not only does she watch the other characters, she is also repeatedly shown framed at a window, looking out over the landscape.

Claudia's move from the periphery to the centre while retaining her role as observer is the key to the film. For she only assumes the central role by remaining an observer. She is not even then the centre of action, but the elusive centre of consciousness. The other characters observe and are observed. Claudia observes, and her observation becomes the film's focus. She is the consciousness of the film, and its conscience. Anna's distress, Giulia's foolishness, Sandro's equivocation are as Claudia sees them. She is the character about whom, externally, we know the least, but whose viewpoint we are most invited to share. It is only near the end that she mentions, in conversation with Patrizia, that she does not come from the same privileged class background as the others in the group, a fact which puts a retrospective gloss on her position throughout.

Unlike the others, Claudia is deeply affected by the loss of Anna. It is she who drives the search forward, forces Sandro to assume his responsibilities. (Only Corrado helps her.) When Sandro turns his attentions to her, she repels him. According to the script (p. 87), she invites the kiss he gives her on the boat shortly after Anna disappears: 'They look at each other for a while, saying nothing. But the intensity of Claudia's stare, a mixture of desire and fear, is such that Sandro makes his decision: he takes the girl in his arms and kisses her.' In the film, however, the relevant shot shows her from behind. She certainly looks at him, but her expression is invisible. It is a characteristically Antonionian moment in which a clue is withheld. Is there desire as well as fear on that face we cannot see? All the audience can be sure of – if that, the moment is so brief and so little prepared for – is that there has been a hesitation and that the hesitation has produced an event.

Claudia repulses Sandro again in the station waiting-room and on the train. But she decides to join him in the interior, following up the lead supplied by the journalist Zuria. That decision can be read as an acceptance, though the audience is still not prepared for what is to follow. She and Sandro drive on towards Noto. They stop in the deserted village, and a straight cut (rather than the dissolve which the film normally uses to separate sequences from each other) provides the transition from the shot of the car leaving the village to the couple making ecstatic love in a field.[12] Psychologically, this abrupt switch can only be motivated retrospectively. Something has happened to change Claudia's attitude, and with this change in her the film alters course. It has reached its turning point.

On the principle of *post hoc propter hoc*,[13] the precipitating cause of the change in Claudia must be the almost metaphysical sense of loneliness provoked by the sight of the deserted village. But the psychological change could have happened earlier. Claudia up to this point has been a detached or irritated observer of the sexual activities of the others, waiting in the square while Sandro and Anna made love in his flat, watching Patrizia let Raimondo put his hand on her breast on the boat, looking on during the scene between Giulia and Goffredo in his studio full of coarsely painted female nudes. 'No landscape,' says Goffredo sententiously, 'is as beautiful as a woman' – a sentiment which Claudia clearly does not share, for however much the film may concentrate on her light body and expressive features, she herself finds solace in landscape.

L'avventura is not a film in which nothing happens, or in which there is no action. But it is a film in which the action is decentred. The action presses in on Claudia, but she is not usually the person who initiates it. Not that she is passive, or vacillating as a character. On the contrary, she shows every sign of knowing what she wants and of how to get it. She is in fact the driving force behind the search for Anna and her affair with Sandro starts when she is ready for it and will survive (if it is to survive) because of her decision. But this is not enough to make her the active centre, and because the film does little to flesh out her motivations, she is not really the psychological centre of the film either. The audience is invited to share her point of view, but this point of view is not fully inhabited. It is the point of view of someone about whom, when it comes down to it, the audience knows very little. This does not make her seem unreal, or unavailable as a focus of sympathy. The trick – the magic – of the film is that Claudia can be everything she is and yet as a character be so lightly sketched.

Monica Vitti played four roles for Antonioni in the early 1960s. Claudia in *L'avventura* was the first. Then in *La notte* (1961) she appears in the last quarter of the film as Valentina, daughter of a rich industrialist; her father is trying to seduce Giovanni (Marcello Mastroianni), a writer, into working for him as tame in-house intellectual, and Valentina's role seems little more than to add a teasing seductiveness of her own to her father's scheme. In *The Eclipse* she is Vittoria, a young woman who works as a translator; at the opening of the film she breaks up with the man she has been living with and she then enters into a frenzied affair with a young stockbroker (played by Alain Delon), which appears to have no future. Finally in *Red Desert* (1964) she plays Giuliana, a housewife with a young son and a not very sympathetic husband; she toys with the idea of opening a shop, she has a brief fling with a visiting friend of her husband's, she seems very distraught throughout, but in the end her life seems to come together again.

The characters she plays in these four films are all quite different. Giuliana in *Red Desert* is palpably neurotic, whereas the other three, although edgy and unpredictable, appear as beacons of sanity in a world in which nothing seems to make much sense. But the characters have at least one intrinsic trait in common and one extrinsic. The intrinsic trait is that they are presented as characters who are trying, however imperfectly, to make sense. In this respect they are, one might say, the same type of person. The extrinsic trait is that in each case the 'person' embodied in the character is one constructed very sketchily. The only background information given about Valentina is that her parents are rich, and all that is shown of her is her flirtation with Giovanni. About Vittoria we know more, but not much. She is a working woman (Claudia and Valentina may have jobs, but not that we are told about); she has a mother (wonderfully played by Valentina Cortese) who plays the stock exchange; she is independent-minded, wary of attachments; and like Claudia in *L'avventura*, she enjoys moments of solitude and communion with nature. For her part, Giuliana cannot avoid attachment, since she has a little boy to look after; we also know that she has been in a mental hospital and that her illness is more substantial than a vague unhappiness or feeling of malaise.

Four different characters, then, played by the same actress, all represented as engaged in a similar quest, and all constructed in a way that accentuates the immediately visible at the expense of explanatory motivation. The method by which these characters are constructed can perhaps best be understood by means of a flash-forward to the film Antonioni made after the Vitti films, *Blowup*.

Thomas (David Hemmings), the central character of *Blowup*, is a fashion photographer. His job is to photograph models, and the model's job is to be photographed as Thomas wishes her. Antonioni is like Thomas. He uses actors and actresses as models. If they look right, pose correctly, move correctly, he shoots the scene. They are not asked to interpret their role and perform it according to their interpretation. In an interview recently broadcast on BBC Arena,[14] Vanessa Redgrave, co-star of *Blowup*, confessed that in the early stages of the making of the film she found this disconcerting. There she was, an experienced and intelligent theatre actress, and all she was asked to do was pose and move in ways dictated by the director's sense of framing and editing. In the end she reconciled herself to what was required, because her professional judgment told her that what she was being asked to do was almost invariably right.

In *L'avventura*, Antonioni was also working with an experienced and intelligent theatre actress, and Vitti, like Redgrave, had to learn to adapt to an unaccustomed and, at first sight, demeaning method of work. Antonioni was also in love with her. Her role was to be the artist's model, to lend her body to the purposes of the work that he intended to create. In so far as film can be compared to writing, Antonioni's films can be described as texts written on the body of the actor. If a comparison with painting is used, then they are like life studies inspired by the model chosen for the picture (and not only, of course the living model, since they, and *L'avventura* in particular, are also inspired by landscape). Vitti provides a brilliant model to whom this style of work can be applied. Her

Monica Vitti with Marcello Mastroianni in *La notte* (1961)

... in *L'eclisse* (1962)

... in *Red Desert* (1964)

... in *The Oberwald Mystery* (1980)

hand movements, her little bursts of laughter, although mechanically elicited, have a quality of spontaneity which belies the method. Moreover, her performance is always 'in character', because the character consists precisely in the things of which she is asked to be the vehicle. The film takes shape and acquires consistency around her ability to lend herself to its purposes. She is, literally, an embodiment.

What is it exactly that she is called on in *L'avventura* to embody? It can, I think, be best described as a vision: not in the intellectual sense of a vision of the world or *Weltanschauung*, but in that, more limited, of a way of seeing. One could go a step further and reduce this way of seeing to a way of looking, or even just a look. Indeed Antonioni's films have been assimilated to the 'école du regard' exemplified by the novels of Alain Robbe-Grillet and other practitioners of the *nouveau roman* and Robbe-Grillet himself has been one of the most perceptive commentators on them.[15]

Antonioni's way of looking in *L'avventura* is marked by a certain externality. The characters' feelings are not directly expressed, whether in the dialogue or through efforts of performance. An idea of what these feelings might be emerges from the way the characters are viewed and the way they are seen to react to what they themselves are shown to be seeing. If a sense of uncertainty pervades the relationships between the characters, it is because nothing is ever confirmed. Looks between the characters are not reciprocated. Only occasionally is the dialogue used to reinforce and anchor an impression created by the movement of the image. The narrative is loosely articulated. Point-of-view shots are few, and the alternation of shot and reverse-shot, with the camera returning to the previous set-up, is very rare indeed, except at the very end. Until the final moment, in which variations of shot and reverse-shot are played out with almost musical precision, camera movement and editing are in a constant process of flux. The camera pans, tracks, reframes, moves to a new position. Events unfold from a series of a camera positions, all of which uncover new details of a scene but none of which conforms to a stable narrative logic enabling the spectator to place events and assign them unequivocal meanings.

Antonioni's method cannot, however, be reduced to a way of looking, a matter of camera placements, movements and cuts devoid of any preconceptions. Although Antonioni is open to what he sees and avoids dramaturgical devices which channel the meaning of what is represented along pre-set lines, he has a particular 'take' on the world which is not that of the eye alone. His is not the empty, or vacated, consciousness of a *nouveau roman* narrator. He constructs characters, not figurations, and they live in a web of social relations, not atomistically divided one from another. His method is both intuitive and sceptical. It is intuitive in the sense that it works from impressions and suggestions. A landscape or an actor's gesture suggests a possibility of meaning, but that meaning is unproven, and intuition is needed to confirm that the realisation of what is suggested will in fact achieve a purpose. And it is sceptical in that it makes no claims to know the unknowable. Intuition can only go so far.

What is going through Claudia's mind at the end of *L'avventura* when she and Sandro are out on the terrace after his deception has been discovered? No words are spoken. Sandro is crying, but she cannot see his face. His faint sobs are perceptible (though obscured for the audience by the music). Her face as she approaches the bench on which he is sitting is composed. Her eyes are downcast. Only the movement of her hand, clutching the back of the bench and then rising to gently caress his shoulders and his hair, gives any indication of the emotion she is feeling. Of the intensity of her feeling there can be no doubt. The script describes her as looking at him as at 'something that gives her infinite pain', and clearly there was an intention to convey this pain and also what the script (p. 129) calls a 'searing despair'. But the economy by which the emotion is conveyed is also an abstinence. So many things could be competing for space in her mind, but the film neither affirms nor speculates. It leaves the movement of the hand to carry the entire weight of what is allowed to be said. That Sandro is guilty of a shameful betrayal is clearly affirmed. That Claudia forgives him is at least implied. But the basis on which she forgives, and the nature of the pain which calls forth this response, is unstated.

The complexity of Claudia's pain at this moment is not difficult for the audience to respond to and to understand. There is no doubting its reality, but it is also, in its reality, undescribable. Partial, moralistic judgments are, of course, possible: she is hurt, and rightly so, by his behaviour; on the other hand, she was foolish to trust him in the first place. The film does not inhibit the making of such judgments, but it does not endorse them either, nor does it invite a total withdrawal of judgment. If it offers a statement it is a second-order one, a statement

The search for Anna becomes the love affair between Sandro and Claudia: the deserted village and the love-making scene (frame stills)

about the limits of what it is possible to say. It speaks through silence. It opens up a space for comprehension to enter, without saying (because it cannot) what that comprehension should be.

Underlying the story of *L'avventura*, therefore, is a vision of human relations, of what they are and of the limits of what can be represented. It is a vision rather than a philosophy because it is founded concretely on an intuition of the visible. But it is a way of seeing, rather than a look, because the sceptical intuition on which it is founded does not preclude intuition of another order, the sense that there is indeed more than the eye can see and that this more, although unknowable, is nevertheless real.[16] Every artist, it could be said, is a Pygmalion, creating an object out of bits and pieces which then, mysteriously, acquires a life of its own. The characters in *L'avventura* are constructed as beings who feel pleasure and pain, who respond in various ways to what is around them. In their moments of pleasure and pain they cease to be elements of a mosaic and come to embody the obscure sense of something that lies beyond.

Antonioni's method, in *L'avventura* and elsewhere, is experimental. Making the film is a process by which the characters become endowed with life and in which an initial intuition – that it might be possible to represent something as being the case, that a girl might disappear, with yet-to-be-foreseen consequences – makes way to another: that this is indeed the case and the consequences are those which the audience experiences through the characters, culminating in Claudia's gesture towards Sandro at the end of the film. A hypothesis is not so much verified as realised. Although the script lays down the broad lines of what the story is to be, and even gives the actors the majority of their lines, realisation takes place only when the action has been filmed on the spot and when what transpires on location is inscribed on film and brought back to the cutting room to take final shape. It is significant that Antonioni likes to shoot in continuity, since it is only when he really knows (through having tested his hypothesis by shooting it) what happens before, that he can proceed to realise what is to happen after. It is significant, too, that the two most crucial moments in the film, the explosion of Claudia and Sandro's love affair and the betrayal-reconciliation at the end, are not exactly as described in the script. In the former case, the decision to make the abrupt cut from the village to the love-making was made only in the editing;[17] and in the latter case the script only offers a statement of intent, that somehow something will be conveyed of Claudia's pain and despair.

Experiments, however, are not conducted in a void. Antonioni's commitment to a method of hypothesis and realisation, where the realisation tests the hypothesis to see if it can be made to reveal more than its premisses strictly imply, also involves some presuppositions about the likelihood of finding one thing rather than another. Although the world of *L'avventura* is fragmented, it resides upon some sort of order. It is socially stratified and it is gendered. As with most of Antonioni's films, the action takes place in a fairly upper-class milieu which floats upon the surface of society, relating to the world beneath it in only the most perfunctory way. In so far as the film lays claim to sociological truth, it is only a small section of society to which this truth would apply. What we see is a class which is decadent and cannibalistic. If the environment in which Anna's father has chosen to spend his retirement is being destroyed, it is people like Ettore who are responsible for the destruction. Sandro, once an idealist, now prostitutes himself willingly, though with occasional pangs of guilty conscience.

In this respect, the world of *L'avventura* is not different from that of *La notte* and *The Eclipse*. Giovanni in *La notte* is a writer, but has no confidence in what he writes, and seems prepared, like Sandro, to sell himself to the highest bidder, a millionaire with an attractive daughter. In *The Eclipse*, Piero (Alain Delon) is a dealer, unmoved by the fate of clients whose savings are wiped out in a stock market crash. The world of capitalism portrayed in all three films is not vicious. It is the way it is, rather as nature is the way it is, and like nature it is not subject to explanation. The difference is that nature is external to people, whereas having a role in relation to the class system is part of what people are, and the characters of the films are members or hangers-on of the capitalist class.

In this world of unexplained power relations, power belongs to men and consciousness to women – though the exercise of power is not shown as particularly effectual or the exercise of consciousness particularly farseeing. This is most striking in *The Eclipse* where the stock market crash happens like a sudden storm. Piero is caught up in the storm, buying and selling frenetically in order to keep himself afloat. Vittoria observes the spectacle with detachment. In *La notte*, while Giovanni attends a launch party for his book, his wife Lidia (Jeanne

Moreau) goes for a long walk around the Milan suburbs, just seeing things (things which, in Antonioni fashion, don't make sense) and experiencing her own powerlessness in the face of them. Later in the film, as the latent crisis in her and Giovanni's marriage come to a head, she is also shown as more self-aware than her husband and more aware of the limits of what can be done to save the relationship. Even the distraught Giuliana, in *Red Desert*, is shown as struggling through to a level of self-awareness denied to any of the men who surround her.

Does this mean that, in Antonioni's films, women are simply wiser than men? Not necessarily. It is rather that their position on the outside, and the role assigned to them of observers of opaque social mechanisms, means that Antonioni's heroines are the focal point of such insight as is offered into the workings of the world. Meanwhile they are themselves the objects of observation. If Antonioni, in *L'avventura* and the films made immediately after it, occupies a female point of view, it is by way of trying it out, creating heroines who represent the mystery of a woman's consciousness. In Antonioni's more male-centred films, most notably in *Identification of a Woman* (1982), but also in *Il grido* and in *Blowup*, the hero finds women a mystery; the women behave in ways which the hero cannot fathom and which seem to conform to a logic of their own to which he must reluctantly submit. No character in *L'avventura* directly expresses this male puzzlement in the face of the feminine. But it is present in the narration, in the way Claudia is framed, watched, her face expressive of unspoken thought. Claudia is a mystery to the man who has narrated her into being. She is not a metaphysical mystery, an embodiment of the 'eternal feminine'. She is just a character played by an actress who the director happened to be in love with. But as a character she has that most desirable of fictional qualities, that of being someone about whom there is always more to be known.

Roland Barthes, in an essay included in the present volume as an appendix, has summed up Antonioni's distinctiveness under three words, *sagesse* (wisdom), *vigilance* (the French word is perhaps best translated as attentiveness), and fragility. Antonioni, Barthes goes on to say, is neither a realist (that is, he does not claim to show the world as it is) nor a moralist (he does not claim to say how it should be). Instead he tries to catch hold of the evanescence of things, to shape the flux in a certain fashion. His films are reflections on, rather than of, the world. It is this which makes him – Barthes again, but others have noted it too – an essentially modern artist. Of all Antonioni's films, *L'avventura* is the one in which his modernity is most boldly expressed.

The most obvious modernity of *L'avventura* is that which is present in its content. It is a story about characters who are recognisably contemporary – then, as now – in a way which is, or certainly was, unusual in the cinema, and not only in Italy. In this respect, along with the early films of the French *nouvelle vague*, it marks a break with the vast bulk of preceding cinema. In the American cinema up to 1960, only Nicholas Ray seems to me to convey a comparable sense of contemporaneity.

But there is more to modernity than the sense of contemporaneity in what is portrayed. The full modernity of *L'avventura* comes into relief when one compares it with two other very successful (commercially, more successful) Italian films of the same year, Visconti's *Rocco and His Brothers* and Fellini's *La dolce vita*. Both of those films are about inadequate adaptation to the modern world. In *Rocco* there is a march of history, in relation to which the characters, most of all Rocco himself, are seen as retarded. *La dolce vita* lacks this progressivist thrust; it shows a world falling apart, becoming decadent. *L'avventura* seems indifferent to either progress or decadence. Its characters are placed fairly and squarely where they are, with no past to return to or future to advance to. Stripped of consoling certainties, existentially alone, they are observed with a meticulousness that takes nothing for granted.

To observe in this way, however, is also to invent, to question, to take position, to be conscious of everything that has to be stripped away in order to make a fresh start. Half a century or more after the modern movement attempted to perform these operations in literature and painting, *L'avventura* does so for the cinema.

6

FORTUNES

After the Cannes premiere on 15 May, the producers held a party. Although the trade press described the occasion as glittering, it must have been a gloomy affair – a bit like the party that Fred Astaire and Cyd Charisse escape from after the show flops in Minnelli's *The Band Wagon*.

When the film's makers woke up the following morning, however, it was to find that while they were asleep a statement had been issued, signed by twenty-five film-makers and critics and datelined 2 a.m., denouncing the behaviour of the audience and affirming their belief in the film. The signatories included directors Roberto Rossellini and François Reichenbach; producer Anatole Dauman; Nelly Kaplan, then assistant to Abel Gance; Janine André Bazin; and critics René Gilson, Robert Benayoun, André S. Labarthe, Lo Duca and Georges Sadoul. As the day went on, more and more people added their names to the list. The statement read:

> Conscious of the exceptional importance of Michelangelo Antonioni's film *L'avventura* and shocked by the display of hostility that it has aroused, the undersigned critics and professionals express to the film's author their unqualified admiration. Confident that others who share their enthusiasm will follow suit, they call on them to declare their support.

The festival jury, chaired by Georges Simenon, faced a problem, in the form of too many potential prizewinners. Besides *L'avventura*, contenders included Grigory Chukrai's *Ballad of a Soldier*, Bergman's *The Virgin Spring*, Fellini's *La dolce vita* and Buñuel's *The Young One*, as well as a number of French films from both new directors and from the veteran Abel Gance. In the final prizegiving, the main prize, the coveted Palme d'Or, was awarded to Fellini's *La dolce vita*. There was no second prize. *L'avventura* was given a consolatory Special Prize by the jury, 'for its remarkable contribution to the search for a new cinematic language'. It also picked up two other prizes, the Prix de la Nouvelle Critique, given by critics, and a prize awarded by the Association of Film and Television Writers. Newspaper and magazine reports from the festival were overwhelmingly, though not universally, favourable. In *Cahiers du cinéma* Jean Domarchi had reservations, but Benayoun in *Positif* declared it the most important film since *Citizen Kane*.[18] It was clear that the damage done by the audience at the premiere was not going to be irreparable, but the film still had to face the test of public release. With *La dolce vita* already on release and Visconti's *Rocco and His Brothers* due to come out in the autumn, *L'avventura's* producers hesitated over the choice of a release date. The film received a censor's certificate in

Marcello Mastroianni in Fellini's *La dolce vita* (1960)

Alain Delon with Paulo Stoppa in Visconti's *Rocco and His Brothers* (1960)

August, but it was not until the autumn that it went on release, opening in Milan in mid-October and in Rome at the beginning of November. It did good but not spectacular business, eventually grossing 340 million lire – considerably less than either *Rocco* (which had made 1,500 million by the end of the 1960–61 season) or *La dolce vita* (which made even more). In Paris, then as now the capital of cinephilia, it opened on 14 September, and ran for twelve weeks in two first-run cinemas, the Vendôme and the Studio Publicis. The Paris audience totalled 127,960, more or less evenly divided between the dubbed and subtitled versions, and a further 87,000 people saw the film in other French cities. Again, in terms of pure box-office, it did less well than either *La dolce vita* (440,000 spectators in Paris alone) or *Rocco* (316,000) but the intensity of response was tremendous. Of the three Italian films of the year which definitively put the Italian cinema back on the world map (the other great domestic success of 1960, Luigi Comencini's *Tutti a casa*, had far less international impact), it was undoubtedly *L'avventura* which spoke most directly to the young metropolitan audience.

At the London Film Festival in November, *L'avventura* was awarded the Sutherland Trophy – which Antonioni was unable to collect in person because in the meantime the film had (quite absurdly) been indicted for obscenity and he had to stay home to fight a legal battle on its behalf. The film was released in Britain at the end of the month to generally good reviews. The consensus of opinion in the 'quality' press was that it was an unusual film but not outrageously difficult or outlandishly avant-garde. Then, as now, the critics struggled to put into words what it was they felt was distinctive about the film. Dissent came mainly from the left, with Clancy Segal (writing in *Time and Tide*) decidedly half-hearted, and Nina Hibbin in the *Daily Worker* roundly declaring that the film left her cold.[19]

In the United States, where the film arrived in April 1961, the consensus was less broad. But it was well reviewed by Hollis Alpert in the *Saturday Review*, by Dwight Macdonald in *Esquire*, and by the anonymous (but far from bland) reviewer in *Time*. Noticeably, however, as the film travelled further from its country of origin, so it acquired more and more the trappings of the art film, destined for minority audiences and limited release. It is therefore worth stressing that in both Italy and France it was not an 'art house' product but one expected to appeal in a wider market, albeit a mainly urban one.

It was on the basis of similar expectations that Antonioni was able, shortly after the completion of *L'avventura*, to obtain production finance for his next film, *La notte*, shot during the summer of 1960 and released in both Italy and France early in 1961. Like *L'avventura*, *La notte* was an Italian–French co-production, but this time the French participation was more important. Commercially, in fact, *La notte* did better than *L'avventura* in both markets, with the French results in particular aided by the presence of Jeanne Moreau as co-star opposite Marcello Mastroianni. A similar pattern was followed for *The Eclipse*, where Alain Delon stars alongside Monica Vitti, adding a welcome dynamism to the proceedings. On the whole the production companies involved, with the exception of Cino Del Duca who stepped in to save *L'avventura* and Cineriz who were the Italian producers of *The Eclipse*, were not among the most prestigious but were companies on the make, looking for breaks in the fluid but burgeoning market for quality production on both sides of the Alps.

La notte and *The Eclipse* are often described as forming a trilogy with *L'avventura* (sometimes *Red Desert* is added to make it a tetralogy). This is not strictly accurate. They are not a trilogy in the sense in which, say, Satyajit Ray's 'Apu trilogy' of *Pather Panchali*, *Aparajito* and *The World of Apu* forms a trilogy, following the same characters or their successors from film to film. But they are films made close together in time; the same actress appears in all three (indeed in all four); and they are similar both in style and in theme. All of them contain moments of dead time in which the camera lingers somewhere while nothing appears to be happening, and all are concerned with the instability of feelings and relationships. All of them, moreover, are about a particular kind of fragility, the fragility of happiness.

Apropos of an earlier film, *Cronaca di un amore*, Antonioni said, 'I believe in happiness: every time anyone asks me about this, I insist on saying that it exists. But I don't believe it is lasting.'[20] The remark is perhaps not entirely appropriate to *Cronaca*, where happiness – in memory or in prospect, let alone in actuality – seems to elude the lovers entirely. But in the films of the early 60s the notion of a happiness which may be elusive but can nevertheless enter and illuminate the characters' lives is a central connecting thread. It is far more marked in these films (including *Red Desert*) than elsewhere in Antonioni's work. Although none of the films of the so-called trilogy has a happy end – Claudia and

Sandro are only dubiously reconciled, Giovanni and Lidia have to accept that there is little love left in their marriage, Piero and Vittoria's affair looks set not to continue – what happens in the course of the films gives the lie to any attempt to construe them as exercises in pessimism, let alone the 'famous' pessimism with which their director is occasionally taxed.

There is, however, one very important difference between *L'avventura* and the films that immediately follow it. *La notte* and *The Eclipse* are both set in cities – Milan and Rome respectively. Partly because of the relatively favourable shooting conditions, they display a technical mastery lacking in *L'avventura*. Composition, lighting, editing emanate a sense of control, of everything being just so as the director willed it. *L'avventura* by contrast was at the mercy of the elements, both in point of fact and in the impression created. The urbanite characters fear the natural environment because it is wayward and uncontrolled. The director could not control it either, and as a result an element of freedom enters. The world of nature is a world of necessity, but it is a changing world, to which the characters can offer changing responses. It is also, in its alienness, a world which allows respite. It is a place in which it is possible to be alone, to measure one's relationship to the outside and discover if being alone is a condition to be feared or to be embraced.

The cityscapes of *La notte* and *The Eclipse* allow no such respite. Although compositionally sparse, they have great density. The man-made urban landscape presses in on the characters. It affirms its presence in blocks of concrete and in glass walls which are not windows out on to the world but mirrors whose reflection is cast back at the viewer.[21] Even where society is absent or fragmented (as during Lidia's long walk through the Milan suburbs in *La notte*), the material environment is a constant reminder of a world that Man has created and man and woman have to live in, like it or not.

Although there is a claustrophobic aspect to Antonioni's urban environments – the glass and concrete of *La notte*, the suffocating smog of *Red Desert* – they have two redeeming features: they are aesthetically transfigured into objects of beauty, and they can be escaped from. The aestheticisation is in itself a form of escape, most notably in *The Eclipse*, where the hooting of car horns has a musical timbre and a pile of breeze blocks takes the form of a sculpture. To be able to see the environment in this way, as something immediately oppressive, but which one can step

Daria Halprin in *Zabriskie Point* (1969)

Maria Schneider in *The Passenger* (1975)

back from in admiration, is a privilege which is granted not only to the spectator but to the characters themselves. And if, even so, the world presses in too close, it is still possible to get away from it, in reality or in the imagination. Vittoria does both in *The Eclipse*, first by mentally transporting herself into the world of the African savannah evoked by photographs in a friend's flat, and then in the trip to Verona airport where a small plane takes her 'beyond the clouds' for a moment of unexpected peace. And in *Red Desert* Giuliana transports herself and her son to an imagined island where the water and the air are clear and in so doing initiates a healing process which will enable her to live intact in her polluted urban reality.

The critical success and satisfactory box-office figures for the 'tetralogy' provided Antonioni with a stepping stone to a different type of film-making in production and distribution terms. Under a deal negotiated by the Italian producer Carlo Ponti, he was now contracted to make three films backed by MGM for international release. These films were *Blowup* (1966), *Zabriskie Point* (1970) and *The Passenger* (1975). Each offered opportunities and constraints different from those he had known in Italy. They have a different look, a different rhythm and, in the absence of Monica Vitti, a different focus from the films of the early 60s. They also had a mixed critical reception (in the case of *Zabriskie Point* a largely negative one, particularly in the USA). But certain constants of the Antonioni universe remain, notably the way that human dramas are played out against an environment which is, literally, elemental. The properties of light, surfaces, spaces and objects, wetness and dryness, transparency and opacity, solidity and evanescence, openness and enclosure continue to be foregrounded. The characters move restlessly through this intensely physical environment, learning to relate to it and to draw strength from it even in its alienness; they learn to relate also to each other, but in transitory, provisional ways. Most of all they learn to live alone with the margin of freedom that is inescapably theirs and theirs alone.

In 1995, at the prompting of Martin Scorsese and a few other enlightened spirits, the Academy of Motion Picture Arts and Sciences gave Antonioni its life-achievement award. He was eighty-one years old, debilitated by a severe stroke suffered a few years before. In spite of the effects of illness, he made the journey to Los Angeles to accept the award, his second trip there in two years, the previous one having been for a retrospective of his work in 1993. The offering and acceptance of the award were a gesture of reconciliation after his struggles with the industry during the making of *Zabriskie Point* fifteen years earlier and its subsequent mauling by the obtuse critical establishment in America. The award was given to a film-maker who, in the normal course of events, might be expected to be at the end of his career. But in Antonioni's case such a quasi-obituary was premature, since at the time he stepped up to accept the award he was hard at work on a new film, his first for over a decade, with the wonderfully pregnant title *Beyond the Clouds*. At the time of writing he is working on another film. Antonioni's ability to surprise is extraordinary. But it is unlikely that any surprise yet in store is greater than the one sprung upon the world in May 1960, when *L'avventura* received its fateful premiere. It can be endlessly, and uselessly, debated whether *L'avventura* is Antonioni's 'best' film. But it is certainly the one which was the turning point, both for its director and for the cinema at large.

APPENDIX: 'DEAR ANTONIONI …' BY ROLAND BARTHES
....

Text of a speech given by Roland Barthes on the occasion of the granting of the 'Archiginnsio d'oro' to Antonioni by the City of Bologna in February 1980. First published in *Roland Barthes, 'Caro Antonioni': con antologia degli scritti di Antonioni sul cinema*, edited by Carlo di Carlo, Bologna, 1980; and subsequently in *Cahiers du Cinéma* no. 311, May 1980. The translation here is from the French text as published in *Cahiers*.

Dear Antonioni …

Nietzsche distinguishes two figures: the priest and the artist. Priests we have aplenty, from every religion or indeed none at all; but artists? I should like, dear Antonioni, to be allowed to borrow some features of your work to enable me to pin down the three forces – or, if you like, the three virtues – which to my mind constitute the artist. I shall name them at once: vigilance, wisdom, and, most paradoxical of all, fragility.

Unlike the priest, the artist is capable of astonishment and admiration; his look may be critical, but it is not accusatory; the artist does not know resentment. It is because you are an artist that your work is open to the Modern. Many people take the Modern to be a standard to be raised in battle against the old world and its compromised values; but for you the Modern is not the static term of a facile opposition; the Modern is on the contrary an active difficulty in following the changes of Time, not just at the level of grand History but at that of the little History of which each of us is individually the measure. Beginning in the aftermath of the last war, your work has thus proceeded, from moment to moment, in a movement of double vigilance, towards the contemporary world and towards yourself. Each of your films has been, at your personal level, a historical experience, that is to say the abandonment of an old problem and the formulation of a new question; this means that you have lived through and treated the history of the last thirty years *with subtlety*, not as the matter of an artistic reflection or an ideological mission, but as a substance whose magnetism it was your task to capture from work to work. For you, contents and forms are equally historical; dramas, you have said, are plastic as much as psychological. The social, the narrative, the neurotic are just levels – pertinences, as they say in linguistics – of the *world as a whole*, which is the object of every artist's work; there is a succession of interests, not a hierarchy. Strictly speaking, the artist, unlike the thinker, does not evolve; he scans, like a very sensitive instrument, the successive novelty which his own history presents him with; your work is not a fixed reflection, but an iridescent surface over which there pass, depending on what catches your eye or what the times demand of you, figures of the Social or the Passions and those of formal innovations, from modes of narration to the use of colour. Your concern for the times you live in is not that of a historian, a politician or a moralist, but rather that of a utopian whose perception is seeking to pinpoint the new world, because he is eager for this world and already wants to be part of it. The vigilance of the artist, which is yours, is a lover's vigilance, the vigilance of desire.

I call the wisdom of the artist, not an antique virtue, still less a discourse of mediocrity, but on the contrary that moral knowing, that discerning sharpness which enables him to distinguish meaning and truth. How many crimes has humanity not committed in the name of Truth! And yet this truth was only ever just a meaning. All those wars, repressions, terrors, genocides, for the sake of the triumph of a meaning!

N.U. (Nettezza Urbana) (1948): street-cleaners

The artist, for his part, knows that the meaning of a thing is not its truth; this knowing is a wisdom – a wisdom of the mad, one might say, because it withdraws him from the community, from the herd of fanatics and the arrogant.

Not all artists, however, possess this wisdom; many make a hypostasis of meaning. This terrorist operation generally goes under the name of realism. So, when you declare (in your interview with Godard[22]), 'I feel the need to express reality, but in terms which are not completely realist,' you show a true sense of meaning: you don't impose it, but you don't abolish it. This dialectic gives your films (and I shall use the same word again) a great subtlety: your art consists in always leaving the road of meaning open and as if undecided – out of scrupulousness. In this respect you accomplish very precisely the task of the artist as our time requires it: neither dogmatic, nor empty of signification. Thus, in your first short films on the Rome street-cleaners or the manufacture of rayon at Torviscosa, the critical description of social alienation vacillates, without giving way, in favour of a more immediate and more pathos-laden sentiment of bodies at work. In *Il grido*, the strong meaning of the work is, one might say, the very uncertainty of meaning. the wandering of a man who cannot find his identity confirmed anywhere and the ambiguity of the conclusion (suicide, accident?) lead the spectator to doubt the meaning of the message. This leakage of meaning, which is not the same as its abolition, enables you to disturb the psychological certitudes of realism. In *Red Desert* the crisis is no longer a crisis of feelings, as it is in *The Eclipse*, since feelings in it are secure (the heroine loves her husband): everything comes together, and hurts, in a second zone where it is affect – the discomfiture of affect – which escapes the grip of meaning at the heart of the identity of events (*Blowup*) or of people (*The Passenger*). Throughout your work, basically, there is a constant critique, at once painful and demanding, of that strong imprint of meaning known as destiny.

This vacillation – or perhaps it would be more accurate to say, *syncope* – of meaning follows technical, specifically filmic paths (décor, shots, montage), which I do not regard myself as competent to analyse. As I see it, I am here to say in what way your work, above and beyond its role as cinema, offers a challenge to all contemporary artists. You work at making *subtle* the meaning of what man says, recounts, sees or feels, and this subtlety of meaning, this conviction that meaning does not stop crudely with the thing being said but always goes further, fascinated by what lies beyond – this subtlety is, I believe, that of all artists, whose object is not this or that technique but that strange phenomenon, vibration. The object represented vibrates, to the detriment of dogma. I think of the words of the painter Braque: 'The painting is finished when it has effaced the idea.' I think of Matisse, drawing an olive tree from his bed, and beginning after a while to observe the voids between the branches and discovering that this new vision enabled him to escape the habitual image of the object being drawn – the cliché 'olive tree'. Matisse thus discovered the principle of oriental art, which always wants to paint the void, or rather which grasps the object to be represented at the precious moment when the fullness of its identity suddenly slips into a new space, that of the interstice. There is a way in which your art is also an art of the interstice (the most striking example of this would be *L'avventura*) and in a way too, therefore, your art has a relationship with the Orient. It was your film on China which made we want to go there, and if this film was initially rejected by those who should have understood that the force of love in it was more valuable than any propaganda, this is because it was judged according to a power reflex

6 6   David Hemmings in *Blowup* (1966)

rather than the demands of truth. The artist has no power, but he has some relationship with truth; his work – always allegorical if it is a great work – approaches truth at an angle; his world is truth seized indirectly.

Why is this subtlety of meaning so crucial? Precisely because meaning, from the moment that it is fixed and imposed and ceases to be subtle, becomes an instrument, a counter in the power game. To make meaning subtle is therefore a second-level political activity, as is any attempt to crumble, disturb or undo the fanaticism of meaning. This is not without its dangers. So the third virtue of the artist (using virtue in its Latin sense[23]) is his fragility: the artist is never confident of living and working. This fact is a simple but serious one; his obliteration is always a possibility.

The first fragility of the artist is this: he is part of a changing world, but he changes too. This is banal, but for the artist it is bewildering, for he never knows if the work he is putting forward is the result of changes in the world or in his subjectivity. You have always been conscious of this relativity of Time, for example when you said in an interview: 'If the things we talk about today are no longer those that we talked about just after the war, this is because the world around us indeed changed, but we have changed too. Our needs, our concerns, our themes have changed.'[24] This fragility is that of an existential doubt which seizes the artist as and when his life and work move on; this doubt is difficult, painful even, for the artist never knows if what he sets out to say bears truthful witness on the world as it has changed or is just an egotistical reflection of his nostalgia or his desire. An Einsteinian traveller, he never knows if it is the train or space-time which is in motion, if he is a witness or a man of desire.

Another aspect of fragility for the artist, paradoxically, is the firmness and insistence of his look. Power of any kind, because it is violence, never looks; if it looked one minute longer (one minute too much) it would lose its essence as power. The artist, for his part, stops and looks lengthily, and I would imagine you became a film-maker because the camera is an eye, constrained by its technical properties to look. What you, like all film-makers, add to these properties is to look at things radically, until you have exhausted them. On the one side you look lengthily at what you were not expected to look at either by political convention (the Chinese peasants) or by narrative convention (the dead times of an adventure). On the other your preferred hero is someone who looks (a photographer, a reporter). This is dangerous, because to look longer than expected (I insist on this added intensity) disturbs established orders of every kind, to the extent that normally the time of the look is controlled by society; hence the scandalous nature of certain photographs and certain films, not the most indecent or the most combative, but just the most 'posed'.

The artist is therefore threatened, not just by established power (the martyrology of artists throughout history censored by the state is chillingly long) but also by a collective feeling, ever latent, that society can do without art. Artistic activity is suspect because it disturbs the comfort and security of established meanings, because it is expensive and yet free, and because the new society in search of itself, whatever the regime it lives under, has not yet decided what it should think about *luxury*. Our fate is uncertain, and this uncertainty does not have a simple relationship with the political solutions we can envisage for the discomfiture of the world; it depends on History on a grand scale, which decides, in a way beyond our understanding, not about our needs but about our desires.

Dear Antonioni, I have tried to set forth in my intellectual language the reasons which make you, over and above the cinema, one of the artists of our time. This compliment is not simple, as you know; for the artist today is in a position no longer supported by the good conscience of a great sacred or social function. Being an artist does not give you a cosy spot in the bourgeois Pantheon of Guiding Lights of Humanity. It means in each work confronting in oneself those spectres of modern subjectivity which are (from the moment one is no longer a priest) ideological lassitude, social bad conscience, the attraction and disgust of facile art, the quivering of responsibility, the constant scruple which leaves the artist strung out between solitude and gregariousness. Today, therefore, you must take advantage of this peaceful, harmonious moment of agreement when a whole collectivity joins together to recognise, admire and love your work. For tomorrow the labour begins again.

NOTES

· ·

1 As Dante puts it in Canto iii of *Inferno*, ' … so long a trail, I had not thought death had undone so many.' For death read 'restructuring'.

2 See Geoffrey Nowell-Smith, 'Away from the Po Valley blues', *Pix* no. 1, 1993, pp. 24–30.

3 With exceptions. Neo-realism had room for films as diverse as Giuseppe De Santis's *Bitter Rice* (1949) with its proletarian subject (labour struggles among migrant workers in the rice fields) and its melodramatic and mannered plot, and Rossellini's *Europa '51* (1952) with its bourgeois setting, spiritualistic ethos, and classically neo-realist economy of means. Needless to say, supporters of one version of neo-realism roundly condemned other versions as not neo-realist.

4 A perceptive contemporary comment was provided by Fernaldo Di Giammatteo in *Bianco e Nero*, April 1951 – extensively quoted in Sam Rohdie, *Antonioni* (London: BFI, 1990). The film was perhaps better appreciated by film-makers (notably in Spain) than by critics or audiences. For more recent studies of the film see Noel Burch, *Theory of Film Practice* (New York: Praeger; and London: Secker & Warburg, 1973), pp. 76–80, and Rohdie, *Antonioni*, pp. 43–56.

5 M. Antonioni, 'Prefazione a *sei film*', in *Fare un film è per me vivere: scritti sul cinema*, edited by Carlo di Carlo and Giorgio Tinazzi (Venice: Marsilio, 1994), p. 57. Originally published in 1964 as a foreword to an edition of the scripts of *Le amiche*, *Il grido*, *L'avventura*, *La notte* and *The Eclipse*.

6 This, and much of the information that follows, is derived from a diary of the shooting included with the published script: *L'avventura*, edited by Tommaso Chiaretti (Bologna: Cappelli, 1960), hereafter referred to simply as 'script'. (The English language version of the script, contained in *Screenplays of Michelangelo Antonioni* (New York: Orion Press, 1963), does not contain this diary or any other supplementary material.)

7 Private communication, Los Angeles, February 1993. In spite of repeated viewings, I have not been able to identify this cutaway, which is supposedly inserted into a scene on a train as Sandro accompanies Claudia on her way to the Lampedusa villa.

8 Script, p. 44.

9 The full screen width is not perfectly visible on the video available in Britain, which is slightly cropped at the edges.

10 According to the script (p. 35), the old man, a real-life inhabitant of Panarea where the cast and crew were lodged, insisted on speaking English so that when the film was released in Australia his family out there could understand him.

11 His words are (my translation): 'Giulia is like Oscar Wilde: give her excess and she will do without the bare necessities.'

12 In the script (p. 111) Sandro and Claudia start touching each other while still in the village and retire to a shady spot just outside where they make love, and the scene was in fact shot that way. In the film, however, no spatial link is established between the village and the field, nor is there any indication of elapsed time. The cut disrupts temporal and spatial continuity, and its effect is dramatic. According to a note in the script (pp. 134–5), the decision to separate the scenes in this abrupt way was taken during the editing, for reasons of economy.

13 'After this, therefore because of this'. A dubious principle in logic, but an essential one in narrative, where events do not only follow each other but result from them. Ordinary narrative is both linear and causal. That is to say, events form a chain: what happens first motivates what happens next, and so through to the end. Understanding the narrative involves a presumption that this causal chain is in fact operative, which it usually is. But because the presumption exists, narratives can also be constructed to go against it. The films of Buñuel, from *Un chien andalou* to *Le Fantôme de la liberté*, are an example of narratives which disconcert the spectator by making apparently unmotivated transitions from one event to another. Antonioni's films do not do this. They preserve at least a semblance of linearity, but causality is weakened.

14 'Dear Antonioni', *Arena*, BBC2, tx. 18 January 1997.

15 See the *Arena* programme. Another 'nouveau romancier', Michel Butor, praised *L'avventura* and *La notte* for their 'way of seeing, of recording life' and for 'the subtlety of the relationship between what is shown and what is said, between the image and the word': quoted in the French edition of the published script of *La notte*: *La Nuit* (Paris: Buchet–Chastel, 1961), pp. 11–12).

16 Rohdie, in the epigraph to his book, quotes Antonioni: 'The world, the reality in which we live ... is invisible, hence we have to be satisfied with what we see.'

17 See note 12 above.

18 In *Cahiers du Cinéma* no. 108, June 1960, and *Positif* no. 35, July–August 1960, respectively.

19 Favourable reviews were in the *Daily Telegraph* (Patrick Gibbs), *Financial Times* (David Robinson), *Evening Standard* (Alexander Walker), *Manchester Guardian* (anonymous), *The Times* (anonymous, but probably John Russell Taylor), *The Spectator* (Isabel Quigley) and of course *Sight and Sound* (Penelope Houston). The negative approach taken by the left was one reason why I felt impelled to defend the film in the new left magazine *New University*.

20 *Positif* no. 30, July 1959, p. 9.

21 An extended treatment of Antonioni's use of glass in *La notte* is to be found in David Bass, 'Window/Glass: reflections on Antonioni', *Scroope* no. 7, 1994/5.

22 *Translator's note. Cahiers du Cinéma* no. 160, November 1964, pp. 8–17.

23 *Translator's note.* The Latin word *virtus* (cognate with *vir*, 'a man') originally had the vitalistic sense of a capacity to do things, and only later assumed the sense of moral virtue or excellence.

24 *Translator's note. Cahiers du Cinéma* no. 160, November 1964.

CREDITS

....

L'avventura

Italy/France
1960
Cannes film festival screening
15 May 1960
First public screening in Italy
29 June 1960
Production Companies
Cino Del Duca Produzioni Cinematografiche Europee (Rome)/Société Cinématographique Lyre (Paris)
Producer
Amato Pennasilico
Production Manager
Luciano Perugia
General Organiser
Angelo Corso
Production Inspectors
Enrico Bologna, Fernando Cinquini
Director
Michelangelo Antonioni
Assistant Directors
Franco Indovina, Gianni Arduini
Second Assistant Director
Jack O'Connell
Screenplay
Michelangelo Antonioni, Elio Bartolini, Tonino Guerra
Story
Michelangelo Antonioni
Script Supervisor
Elvira D'Amico
Director of Photography
Aldo Scavarda
Camera Operator
Luigi Kuveiller

Music
Giovanni Fusco
Editor
Eraldo Da Roma
Art Director
Piero Poletto
Costumes
Adriana Berselli
Make-up
Ultimo Peruzzi
Hairdresser
Mario Mandini
Stills
Enrico Appetito
Sound Technician
Claudio Maielli
Sound Mixers
P. Ketoff, Fausto Ancillai, Nino Renda
142.5 minutes
12830 feet

Gabriele Ferzetti
Sandro
Monica Vitti
Claudia
Lea Massari
Anna
Dominique Blanchar
Giulia
Renzo Ricci
Anna's father
James Addams
Corrado
Dorothy De Poliolo
Gloria Perkins
Lelio Luttazzi
Raimondo
Giovanni Petrucci
Goffredo, young painter
Esmeralda Ruspoli
Patrizia
Angela Tommaso Di Lampedusa
Princess
Jack O'Connell
pretentious man in art gallery
Enrico Bologna

Franco Cimino
Giovanni Danesi
Rita Molè
Renato Pinciroli
Vincenzo Tranchina

Credits checked by Markku Salmi

L'avventura is available in Britain in 35 mm from the BFI and on sell-through video from Connoisseur Video. In the United States it also exists on laserdisc, in the Criterion Collection, with commentary by Gene Youngblood.

The print of *L'avventura* in the National Film and Television Archive was acquired specially for the 360 Classic Feature Films project through La Société Cinématographique, Paris.

Feature-length films by Antonioni
(The original title is given first, in bold, followed in the case of co-productions by the release title in the second co-producing country. English-language titles are in brackets – release titles in italics, translations of the original title in quotation marks.)

Cronaca di un amore ('Story of a love affair'), Italy 1950
I vinti/Les Vaincus ('The vanquished', sometimes known as *These Our Children*), Italy/France 1952
La signora senza camelie ('The lady without camellias'), Italy 1953
Le amiche ('The girlfriends'), Italy 1955
Il grido/The Cry, Italy/USA 1957
L'avventura ('The adventure'), Italy/France 1960
La notte/La Nuit ('The night'), Italy/France 1961
L'eclisse/L'Éclipse (*The Eclipse*), Italy/France 1962

Il deserto rosso/Le Désert rouge (*Red Desert*), Italy/France 1964
Blowup, GB/Italy 1966
Zabriskie Point, USA 1969
Chung Kuo Cina, Italy 1972
Professione: Reporter/El reporter (*The Passenger*), Italy/Spain 1975
Il mistero di Oberwald (*The Oberwald Mystery*), Italy 1980
Identificazione di una donna / Identification d'une femme (*Identification of a Woman*), Italy/France 1982
Par delà les nuages / Al di là delle nuvole (*Beyond the Clouds*), France/Italy 1995

BIBLIOGRAPHY

· ·

The English-language bibliography on
L'avventura is scant. On Antonioni's work in
general there are three recent books: Seymour
Chatman, *Antonioni, or The Surface of the
World* (Berkeley: University of California
Press, 1985); Sam Rohdie, *Antonioni* (London:
BFI, 1990) and William Arrowsmith,
Antonioni: The Poet of Images, ed. Ted Perry
(Oxford: OUP, 1995). Rohdie's is by far the
most insightful: unfortunately it does not deal
with *L'avventura* in particular detail. Chatman
is relatively good on *L'avventura*, but is let
down by an antipathy and incomprehension
towards Antonioni's later films.

Two long out-of-print monographs are Ian
Cameron and Robin Wood, *Antonioni*
(London: Studio Vista, 1968) and Philip
Strick, *Antonioni* (Loughton, Essex: Motion
Publications, 1963). Both are useful, but suffer
from a temptation to over-interpret.

My essay on *L'avventura* and *The Eclipse*,
published under the title 'Shape around a
black point' in *Sight and Sound*, Winter 1963/
64 (reprinted, shorn of its illustrations, in B.
Nichols, ed., *Movies and Methods*, Berkeley:
University of California Press, 1976),
attempts to protect the films from excesses of
interpretation. Its argument still seems to me
valid.

The literature in Italian and French is far
richer. Much of it is scattered in journals,
especially *Cahiers du Cinèma* and *Positif*. A
good selection of articles from various sources
is to be found in two volumes (in French)
published by the Ente autonomo per la
gestione del cinema in Rome in 1987 and 1988:
Michelangelo Antonioni, 1942/1965, edited by
Carlo di Carlo; and *Michelangelo Antonioni,
1966/1984*, edited by Lorenzo Cuccu. Two
very fine books in Italian from the 1970s are:
Lorenzo Cuccu, *La visione come problema*
(Rome: Bulzoni, 1973) and Giorgio Tinazzi
Michelangelo Antonioni (Il Castoro, 1974).
Interesting visual materials are to be found in
Michele Mancini and Giuseppe Perrella,
*Michelangelo Antonioni: architetture della
visione* (Rome: Coneditor, 1986).

The finest thing ever written on Antonioni,
however, is in my opinion, the short text by
Roland Barthes, 'Cher Antonioni …',
published as an appendix to this volume.

The shooting script of *L'avventura* was
published as *L'avventura di Michelangelo
Antonioni*, edited by Tommaso Chiaretti
(Bologna: Cappelli, 1960). The English-
language version of the same script, contained
in *Screenplays of Michelangelo Antonioni* (New
York: Orion Press, 1963) should be used with
caution, since it gives no indication of which
scenes were actually shot as scripted.

ALSO PUBLISHED

If you would like further information about future BFI Film Classics or about other books on film, media and popular culture from BFI Publishing, please write to:

**BFI Film Classics
BFI Publishing
21 Stephen Street
London W1P 2LN**

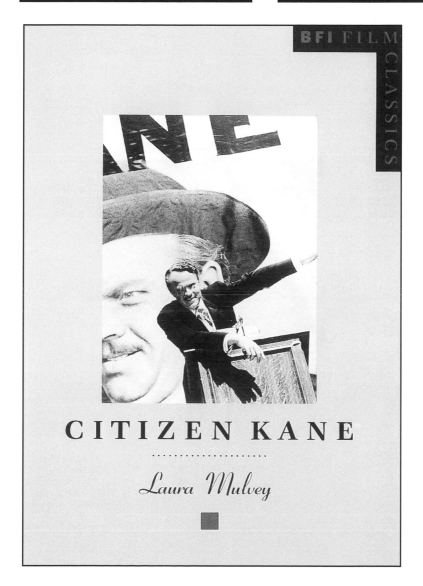

CITIZEN KANE

·····················

Laura Mulvey

"An enthralling account of the movie by one of our best film theorists"
THE GUARDIAN

SINGIN' IN THE RAIN

· · · · · · · · · · · · · · · · · · · ·

Peter Wollen

"Fascinating"
TIME OUT

BFI FILM

CLASSICS

ROCCO

AND HIS BROTHERS

(ROCCO E I SUOI FRATELLI)

· · · · · · · · · · · · · · · · · · · ·

Sam Rohdie

DAS CABINET DES
DR. CALIGARI

. . . .

David Robinson

BFI Film Classics '... could scarcely be improved upon ... informative, intelligent, jargon-free companions.'
The Observer

Each book in the BFI Publishing Film Classics series honours a great film from the history of world cinema. With new titles published each year, the series is rapidly building into a collection representing some of the best writing on film. If you would like to receive further information about future Film Classics or about other books on film, media and popular culture from BFI Publishing, please fill in your name and address and return this card to the BFI*.

No stamp is needed if posted in the UK, Channel Islands, or Isle of Man.

NAME

ADDRESS

POSTCODE

*North America: Please return your card to:
Indiana University Press, Attn: LPB, 601 N Morton Street,
Bloomington, IN 47401-3797

36

**BFI Publishing
21 Stephen Street
FREEPOST 7
LONDON
W1E 4AN**